Air Fryer Cookbook for Beginners with Pictures

Quick & Easy Air Fryer Recipes
with Step-by-Step Instructions for Busy People

The Complete Time-Saving Book
to Cook Everyday Meals

CECILY GOODWIN

DEDICATION

Take care of yourself and always prioritize your well-being.
May you and your family be safe, healthy,
and blessed with all the best life has to offer!

DISCLAIMER

CONTENTS

INTRODUCTION

Welcome to the world of air frying! As we continue to embrace the rapid advancements in kitchen technology, the air fryer has emerged as a revolutionary tool transforming how we cook and enjoy our meals. This modern appliance offers a healthier, quicker, and more efficient way to prepare delicious food, making it an essential addition to any kitchen.

Why has the air fryer become such a beloved kitchen gadget? The secret lies in its ability to cook food with hot air, significantly reducing the need for oil while delivering that irresistible crispy texture we all love. Whether you are a seasoned chef or a beginner in the kitchen, the air fryer opens a world of culinary possibilities that are both easy and exciting. Additionally, you'll discover numerous tips and tricks that will enhance your cooking experience with an air fryer.

The good news is that you can air-fry all kinds of food. I've prepared a wide variety of recipes with colorful pictures for you. From classic comfort foods to innovative dishes, each recipe is designed to help you make the most of this amazing appliance. You'll discover how to air fry everything from poultry and seafood to desserts and snacks, all with minimal fuss and maximum flavor.

Let's get started!

HOW DOES THE AIR FRYER WORK?

This device uses Rapid Air Technology, which combines a heating element and a powerful fan to circulate hot air around the food in a perforated cooking basket. The heating element quickly reaches high temperatures, while the fan ensures that the hot air is distributed evenly and rapidly around the food, promoting even cooking. This setup allows the air fryer to cook food efficiently and achieve a crispy exterior like deep frying.

The perforated cooking basket design ensures that the hot air reaches every part of the food, resulting in a uniform texture and flavor. The air fryer also uses significantly less oil than traditional frying methods, often requiring just a light coating or spray of oil. With adjustable temperature and timer controls, the air fryer provides precise cooking for various types of food, making it a healthier and convenient alternative to traditional frying methods.

ANATOMY OF AN AIR FRYER

Heating Element
Located at the top, it generates the heat needed to cook the food.

Fan
Above the heating element, it circulates hot air around the food for even cooking and a crispy finish.

Cooking Basket
The main compartment where food is placed, usually perforated to allow air to flow freely around the food.

Drip Tray
It catches grease and food particles beneath the cooking basket, making cleanup easier.

Control Panel
Found on the front, it includes buttons or a touchscreen for setting the temperature, time, and cooking modes, with some models offering pre-programmed settings.

Air Intake and Exhaust

Air intake vents draw in air, while exhaust vents release hot air and steam, ensuring proper ventilation and preventing overheating.

Safety Mechanisms

Built-in safety features like overheat protection, automatic shut-off, and cool-touch handles ensure safe operation.

Exterior Housing

The outer shell is designed to stay relatively cool to the touch, providing insulation to keep the heat inside and protect users from burns.

Accessories

Additional items like baking pans, racks, skewers, and silicone mats increase the air fryer's versatility, allowing for a wider range of cooking methods.

THE ADVANTAGES OF AIR FRYING

Easy and Safe to Use

Air fryers are user-friendly, featuring simple controls and safety mechanisms that make them accessible even for novice cooks. The enclosed cooking system minimizes the risk of hot oil splatters, reducing potential kitchen accidents.

Crisp, Crunchy Food with Minimal Oil

One of the most significant advantages of an air fryer is its ability to make crispy and crunchy foods with significantly less oil than traditional frying methods. This not only makes your meals healthier but also reduces the mess associated with deep frying.

Versatile

Air fryers are incredibly versatile kitchen appliances. In addition to frying, they can bake, roast, and grill, allowing you to prepare a wide variety of dishes, from chicken wings and crispy fries to roasted vegetables and even desserts.

Cook Faster

These devices use rapid air technology to cook meals quickly and evenly. This efficiency means you can prepare food in a fraction of the time it would take using conventional ovens or stovetops.

Make Healthier Meals

By using little to no oil, air fryers help reduce the fat content in your dishes, making them a healthier option. You can indulge in your favorite fried foods, consuming fewer calories and guilt.

A Wide Variety of Options

With an air fryer, you can cook a wide range of recipes. The possibilities are endless, from main courses and appetizers to desserts or snacks, making it a valuable addition to any kitchen.

Energy Saving

Air fryers are more energy-efficient than traditional ovens. They heat up quickly and cook food faster, which helps reduce overall energy consumption and can lower electricity bills.

AIR FRYER TIPS & TRICKS

Preheat Your Air Fryer

Like an oven, preheating your air fryer for a few minutes before adding your food ensures that it reaches the needed cooking temperature faster and cooks your food more evenly.

Avoid Overcrowding

For better results, avoid overcrowding the basket. Spread your food in a single layer to allow hot air to circulate freely, ensuring even cooking and crispiness.

Shake or Flip Halfway Through

For even cooking, especially with smaller items like fries or vegetables, shake the basket or flip the food halfway through the cooking time.

Use a Light Coating of Oil

While air fryers use much less oil than traditional frying, a light oil coating can help achieve that crispy texture. Use any brush or spray bottle to apply a thin layer of oil over your ingredients.

Adjust Cooking Times and Temperatures

Air fryers usually cook food faster than traditional ovens. Start from the recommended time and temperature, but be prepared to adjust them based on your specific model and the food you're cooking.

Line the Basket for Easy Cleanup

Line the basket with aluminum foil or parchment paper, ensuring that it does not block air vents. This action will make cleanup easier, especially when cooking items that might stick or drip.

Clean Regularly and Keep It Dry

Pat dry foods like meats and vegetables before air frying to avoid excess moisture, which can prevent achieving a crispy finish.

HOW TO CLEAN THE AIR FRYER?

Keeping your air fryer clean is essential for maintaining its performance and ensuring your food tastes great.

For deep cleaning, you need to be more careful and follow instructions. Let's start with the list of things you will need:

- Damp microfiber cloth
- Soft-bristle scrub brush
- Baking soda
- Dish soap
- Dry, clean cloth

Now, follow the below instructions:

1. **Prepare for Cleaning**
   - Turn off and unplug the air fryer. Allow it to cool completely before cleaning.
   - Open the air fryer and remove all removable parts, such as the basket, tray, and racks.
2. **Clean Removable Parts**
   - Wash the basket, tray, and racks with warm, soapy water. Scrub any food residue with a damp cloth or sponge.
   - Rinse thoroughly with clean water and dry with a soft cloth. Some parts may be dishwasher-safe, so refer to your owner's manual for specific instructions.
3. **Clean the Interior**
   - Wipe down the interior surfaces of the device with a soft cloth. Take a damp cloth with warm water and dish soap for tough spots, and gently scrub.
   - Avoid using abrasive or harsh cleaning agents that could damage the nonstick coating.
4. **Clean the Exterior**
   - Wipe the exterior of the air fryer with a clean, damp cloth and then dry thoroughly.
   - Make sure to clean around the buttons and display area gently to avoid damage.
5. **Reassemble the Air Fryer**
   - Once all parts are thoroughly dry, reassemble the air fryer. Ensure that everything is correctly positioned and securely in place.

Clean your air fryer after each use to prevent flavor mixing and to keep it in optimal working condition.

Following these simple steps will keep your air fryer clean and ready to cook the next delicious meal!

AIR FRYER CONVERSION

If you want to change the oven-cooked recipes to be suitable for air-frying, you need to follow Mason's general rule of thumb. The rule is to reduce the temperature by 25°F and cut the time of cooking by about 20%.

Please, use the pause button on the air fryer from time to time and check your food's readiness. If it is necessary, you should flip the food on the other side to achieve crispness evenly.

COOKING TIME

Oven Time	Air Fryer Time
10 minutes	8 minutes
15 minutes	12 minutes
20 minutes	16 minutes
25 minutes	20 minutes
30 minutes	24 minutes
35 minutes	28 minutes
40 minutes	32 minutes
45 minutes	36 minutes
50 minutes	40 minutes
55 minutes	44 minutes
1 hour	48 minutes

COOKING TEMPERATURE

Oven	Oven (Fan)	Air Fryer
375°F (190°C)	340°F (170°C)	300°F (150°C)
400°F (200°C)	355°F (180°C)	320°F (160°C)
410°F (210°C)	375°F (190°C)	340°F (170°C)
430°F (220°C)	390°F (200°C)	355°F (180°C)
445°F (230°C)	410°F (210°C)	375°F (190°C)
465°F (240°C)	430°F (220°C)	390°F (200°C)
475°F (245°C)	440°F (225°C)	400°F (205°C)

AIR FRYER COOKING CHART

VEGETABLES

	Temp (°F)	Time (mins)		Temp (°F)	Time (mins)
Asparagus (sliced 1-inch)	400°F	5	Onions (pearl)	400°F	10
Beets (whole)	400°F	40	Parsnips (½-inch chunks)	380°F	15
Broccoli (florets)	400°F	6	Peppers (1-inch chunks)	400°F	15
Brussels sprouts (halved)	380°F	15	Potatoes (small baby, 1.5 lbs)	400°F	15
Carrots (sliced ½ – inch)	380°F	15	Potatoes (1-inch chunks)	400°F	12
Cauliflower (florets)	400°F	12	Potatoes (baked whole)	400°F	40
Corn on the cob	390°F	6	Squash (½-inch chunks)	400°F	12
Eggplant (1 ½-inch cubes)	400°F	15	Sweet potato (baked)	380°F	30-35
Fennel (quartered)	370°F	15	Tomatoes (cherry)	400°F	4
Green beans	400°F	5	Tomatoes (halves)	350°F	10
Kale leaves	250°F	12	Zucchini (½-inch sticks)	400°F	12
Mushrooms (sliced ¼-inch)	400°F	5			

CHICKEN

	Temp (°F)	Time (mins)		Temp (°F)	Time (mins)
Breasts, bone-in (1.25 lbs)	370°F	25	Legs, bone-in (1.75 lbs)	380°F	30
Breasts, boneless (4 oz.)	380°F	12	Wings (2 lbs.)	400°F	12
Drumsticks (2.5 lbs)	370°F	20	Game hen (halved – 2 lbs)	390°F	20
Thighs, bone-in (2 lbs)	380°F	22	Whole chicken	360°F	75
Thighs, boneless (1.5 lbs)	380°F	18-20	Tenders	360°F	8-10

BEEF

	Temp (°F)	Time (mins)		Temp (°F)	Time (mins)
Burger (4 oz.)	370°F	16-20	Meatballs (3-inch)	380°F	10

	Temp (°F)	Time (mins)		Temp (°F)	Time (mins)
Filet mignon (8 oz.)	400°F	18	Ribeye, bone-in (1-inch, 8 oz.)	400°F	10-15
Flank steak (1.5 lbs)	400°F	12	Sirloin steaks (1-inch, 12 oz.)	400°F	9-14
London broil (2 lbs)	400°F	20-28	Beef Eye Round Roast (4 lbs.)	400°F	45-55
Meatballs (1-inch)	370°F	7			

PORK AND LAMB

	Temp (°F)	Time (mins)		Temp (°F)	Time (mins)
Loin (2 lbs.)	360°F	55	Bacon (thick cut)	400°F	6-10
Pork chops (1-inch, 6.5 oz.)	400°F	12	Sausages	380°F	15
Tenderloin	370°F	15	Lamb loin chops (1-inch thick)	400°F	8-12
Bacon (regular)	400°F	5-7	Rack of lamb (1.5 – 2 lbs.)	380°F	22

FISH AND SEAFOOD

	Temp (°F)	Time (mins)		Temp (°F)	Time (mins)
Calamari (8 oz.)	400°F	4	Tuna steak	400°F	7-10
Fish fillet (1-inch, 8 oz.)	400°F	10	Scallops	400°F	5-7
Salmon, fillet (6 oz.)	380°F	12	Shrimp	400°F	5
Swordfish steak	400°F	10	Crab cakes	400°F	10
Lobster tails	370°F	5-7			

FROZEN FOODS

	Temp (°F)	Time (mins)		Temp (°F)	Time (mins)
Onion rings (12 oz.)	400°F	8	Fish sticks (10 oz.)	400°F	10
Thin french fries (20 oz.)	400°F	14	Fish fillets (½-inch, 10 oz.)	400°F	14
Thick french fries (17 oz.)	400°F	18	Chicken nuggets (12 oz.)	400°F	10
Mozzarella sticks (11 oz.)	400°F	8	Breaded shrimp	400°F	9
Pot stickers (10 oz.)	400°F	8	Buffalo wings	400°F	12-15

AIR

FRYER

RECIPES

EGG ROLLS

🕐 35 Min   🍽 18 Egg Rolls

Ingredients

- 3 cups of fresh bean sprouts
- 2 cups of hot water
- 1 pound of ground chicken
- 1 package (14 ounces) of coleslaw mix
- 1 package (10 ounces) of unfrozen and squeezed chopped spinach
- 18 egg roll wrappers
- 1 jar (11 ounces) of barbecue sauce
- 6 chopped green onions
- 3 minced garlic cloves
- 1 tablespoon of minced fresh ginger root
- 1 tablespoon of soy sauce or fish sauce

Cooking Instructions

1. Soak bean sprouts for 5 minutes, then drain. Cook chicken with ginger, garlic, green onions, and sauces. Cook spinach, coleslaw, and sprouts, mix with chicken, and cool.
2. Preheat your air fryer to 400°F (205°C). Fill and roll egg wrappers. Air fry in a greased basket for 12-16 minutes, turning once.
3. Serve with barbecue sauce. Enjoy your Egg Rolls!

Useful Tips

You can make the filling for the egg rolls a day or two ahead of time. Store the cooked Egg Rolls in the fridge for up to 4 days.

Nutrition Facts for 1 Egg Roll

Calories: 187 Kcal, Protein: 9 g, Fat: 3 g, Carbohydrates: 9 g, Sugar: 7 g, Cholesterol: 20 mg, Sodium: 388 mg.

BROCCOLI & SALMON QUICHE

🕐 40 Min   🍽 1 Serving

Ingredients

- 1/2 pound of salmon fillet, cut into pieces
- 4 tablespoons of heavy cream
- 4-5 broccoli florets
- 1 large egg, beaten
- 1 tablespoon of grated Cheddar cheese

Cooking Instructions

1. In a mixing bowl, thoroughly whisk together heavy cream and egg.
2. Lightly coat a 5-inch ceramic quiche dish with nonstick cooking spray. Spread the broccoli florets evenly across the bottom of the dish, then add the salmon pieces on top. Pour the prepared egg mixture over the salmon and broccoli, and sprinkle grated Cheddar cheese over everything.
3. Preheat your air fryer to 350°F (180°C). Place the quiche in a suitable basket or baking dish for your air fryer. Cook for 12-15 minutes or until the top is golden brown and the filling is firm.
4. Serve and enjoy your Broccoli & Salmon Quiche!

Useful Tips

Check for doneness by inserting a toothpick into the center; it should come out clean.
Store the cooked quiche in the refrigerator. It will keep well for 3 to 4 days.

Nutrition Facts for 1 Serving

Calories: 298 Kcal, Protein: 17 g, Fat: 25 g, Carbohydrates: 3 g, Sugar: 1 g, Cholesterol: 262 mg, Sodium: 198 mg.

FLUFFY PANCAKES

🕐 40 Min   🍴 16 Pancakes

Ingredients

- 2 cups of all-purpose flour
- 2 cups of buttermilk*
- 2 large eggs
- 2 tablespoons of melted butter
- 2 tablespoons of vanilla extract
- 2 tablespoons of sugar
- 1 tablespoon of baking powder
- 1 tablespoon of baking soda
- 1/4 tablespoon of salt

Cooking Instructions

1. Combine eggs, buttermilk, melted butter, and vanilla, then sift in dry ingredients and mix until smooth; let rest for 20 minutes.
2. Grease silicone molds, add batter to each mold, and air fry at 350°F (180°C) for 5 minutes; flip and cook for 4 more minutes, repeating with remaining batter.
3. Serve with maple syrup, fresh berries, or your favorite toppings. Enjoy your Fluffy Pancakes!

Useful Tips

* Buttermilk is ideal for fluffy pancakes due to its acid reaction with baking soda. If you don't have buttermilk, add sour cream or yogurt with lemon juice for similar results.

Store the cooked pancakes in the refrigerator. It will keep well for 2-3 days.

Nutrition Facts for 1 Pancake

Calories: 103 Kcal, Protein: 3 g, Fat: 3 g, Carbohydrates: 15 g, Sugar: 3 g, Cholesterol: 28 mg, Sodium: 156 mg.

BACON & EGG CUPS

🕐 35 Min   🍴 8 Cups

Ingredients

- 4 large eggs
- 4 strips of bacon
- 1/2 cup of shredded cheddar cheese
- 1/3 cup of half-and-half cream
- 2 chopped green onions
- 1/8 teaspoon of pepper

Cooking Instructions

1. Cook bacon strips in a skillet over medium heat until cooked but not crisp, then drain on paper towels and keep warm. Preheat air fryer to 350°F (180°C). Whisk together half-and-half cream, eggs, and pepper. Wrap bacon around the inside edges of two 8-ounce ramekins coated with cooking spray.
2. Sprinkle half of the cheese and green onions into the ramekins, then divide the egg mixture between them. Crack each remaining egg into the ramekins and sprinkle with the remaining cheese and green onions. Place the ramekins on a tray in the air fryer basket and cook for 15-20 minutes until the eggs are set. Let stand for 5 minutes before serving.
3. Serve and enjoy your Bacon & Egg Cups!

Useful Tips

Store the cooked cups in the refrigerator. It will keep well for 2-3 days.

Nutrition Facts for 1 Cup

Calories: 50 Kcal, Protein: 4 g, Fat: 4 g, Carbohydrates: 1 g, Sugar: 0 g, Cholesterol: 55 mg, Sodium: 80 mg.

VEGETABLE FRITTATA

🕐 27 Min   🍽 2 Servings

Ingredients

- 1 cup of chopped fresh spinach
- 1/4 cup of chopped red bell pepper
- 2 sliced green onions
- 6 eggs
- 2 tablespoons of your favorite shredded cheese (such as Parmesan, Cheddar, Mozzarella)
- 2 tablespoons of milk
- Kosher salt, to taste
- Black pepper, to taste

Cooking Instructions

1. Whisk the eggs in a large bowl until beaten, then add milk, chopped spinach, bell pepper, green onion, salt, and pepper. Line the air fryer basket with parchment paper, pour the egg mixture into it, and sprinkle the top with shredded cheese.
2. Set the air fryer to 350°F (180°C) and cook for 17 minutes. Remove when the frittata is fully set and golden brown.
3. Serve and enjoy your Vegetable Frittata!

Useful Tips

To avoid the frittata sticking to the parchment paper or air fryer basket, generously spray the parchment paper with non-stick cooking spray before pouring in the egg mixture.
Store in the refrigerator. It will keep well for 2-3 days.

Nutrition Facts for 1 Serving

Calories: 267 Kcal, Protein: 21 g, Fat: 17 g, Carbohydrates: 5 g, Sugar: 3 g, Cholesterol: 567 mg, Sodium: 678 mg.

FRENCH TOAST STICKS

🕐 15 Min   🍽 4 Servings

Ingredients

- 5 slices of bread
- 1/3 cup of milk
- 3 tablespoons of sugar
- 2 tablespoons of flour
- 2 eggs
- 1 teaspoon of ground cinnamon
- 1/2 teaspoon of vanilla extract
- 1/8 teaspoon of salt
- Confectioners' sugar for dusting
- Maple syrup for dipping

Cooking Instructions

1. Preheat your air fryer to 370°F (190°C). Cut each bread slice into 3 pieces.
2. In a wide, shallow dish, combine flour, sugar, ground cinnamon, vanilla extract, salt, eggs, and milk. Whisk until smooth.
3. Dip each bread piece into the egg mixture, coating all sides. Place a round piece of parchment paper in the air fryer and arrange the coated bread pieces in a single layer on top.
4. Cook for about 10 minutes, flipping halfway through.
5. Serve warm with maple syrup and enjoy your French Toast Sticks!

Useful Tips

Store in the refrigerator. It will keep well for 2-3 days.

Nutrition Facts for 1 Serving

Calories: 203 Kcal, Protein: 8 g, Fat: 4 g, Carbohydrates: 33 g, Sugar:12 g, Cholesterol: 95 mg, Sodium: 300 mg.

CASEROLE

🕐 25 Min   🍽 8 Servings

Ingredients

- 1 roll of crescent dough
- 1 cup of cooked ground sausage*
- 4 large eggs
- 1 cup of shredded cheddar cheese

Cooking Instructions

1. Coat your baking pan with cooking spray.
2. Spread the crescent dough evenly in the pan, pinching the seams closed with your fingers. Place the pan in the air fryer and cook at 305°F (155°C) for 4-6 minutes, until the dough is golden brown.
3. In a small bowl, beat the eggs until smooth.
4. Distribute the cooked ground sausage evenly over the baked dough, then pour the beaten eggs on top.
5. Put the pan back into the air fryer and cook for another 4 to 8 minutes at 305°F (150°C) until the eggs are set.
6. Once the eggs are firm, sprinkle the shredded cheddar cheese on top.
7. Serve and enjoy your Casserole!

Useful Tips

* Choose your favorite breakfast sausage, whether pork, turkey or a meatless option, for a savory protein boost.
Store in the refrigerator. It will keep well for 2-3 days.

Nutrition Facts for 1 Serving

Calories: 180 Kcal, Protein: 11 g, Fat: 15 g, Carbohydrates: 1 g, Sugar: 1 g, Cholesterol: 127 mg, Sodium: 309 mg.

BACON & CHEESE SANDWICH

🕐 20 Min   🍽 1 Sandwich

Ingredients

- 2 fried eggs, seasoned to taste
- 3 to 4 pieces of thick-cut bacon
- 2-4 slices of cheddar cheese
- 2 slices of light bread
- 1 tablespoon of butter or mayo for toasting the bread
- 1 teaspoon of mayonnaise*, optional

Cooking Instructions

1. Cook the bacon slices in the air fryer at 350-375°F (180-190°C) for 3-6 minutes until crispy, then set aside. Spread butter or mayo on one side of each bread slice.
2. Fry eggs in a skillet or air fryer, flipping once to cook both sides.
3. Assemble the sandwich: place one slice of cheese on the bread, add the fried egg, another slice of cheese, the crispy bacon, and a final slice of cheese. Top with the second bread slice.
4. Air fry the sandwich for 1-2 minutes until toasted.
5. Serve and enjoy your Bacon & Cheese Sandwich!

Useful Tips

* Use your favorite vegan cheddar instead if you want to keep it plant-forward.
Store in the refrigerator. It will keep well for 3 days.

Nutrition Facts for 1 Sandwich

Calories: 935 Kcal, Protein: 49 g, Fat: 69 g, Carbohydrates: 31 g, Sugar: 6 g, Cholesterol: 539 mg, Sodium: 1748 mg.

HASH BROWNS

🕐 55 Min   🍴 15 Hashbrowns

Ingredients

- 4 large russet potatoes
- 2 teaspoons of vegetable oil
- 2 tablespoons of breadcrumbs
- 2 teaspoons of kosher salt
- 1 teaspoon of garlic powder
- 1 teaspoon of onion powder
- 1 teaspoon of ground black pepper

Cooking Instructions

1. Gather the ingredients. Peel, shred and soak the potatoes in cold water for 10-20 minutes. Drain, rinse, and microwave for 4-5 minutes, stirring every minute. Pat dry.
2. Mix the potatoes with breadcrumbs, 1 teaspoon salt, pepper, garlic powder, and onion powder. Form patties using an egg mold or cookie cutter on a parchment-lined baking sheet. Refrigerate for 20 minutes. Preheat the air fryer to 360°F (185°C).
3. Brush the basket with some oil and place the patties in a single layer. Air fry for 15 minutes, flipping halfway, until golden brown.
4. Sprinkle with remaining salt and serve immediately. Enjoy your Hash Browns!

Useful Tips

You can store these hash browns in the fridge, wrapped in foil, for up to 3 days. Reheat them in the air fryer for a few minutes before serving.

Nutrition Facts for 3 Hashbrowns

Calories: 63 Kcal, Protein: 7 g, Fat: 2 g, Carbohydrates: 54 g, Sugar: 3 g, Cholesterol: 0 mg, Sodium: 900 mg.

STUFFED PEPPERS

🕐 18 Min   🍴 2 Servings

Ingredients

- 4 eggs
- 1 bell pepper, halved with seeds removed
- 1 teaspoon of olive oil
- 1 pinch salt and pepper
- 1 pinch of sriracha flakes, optional

Cooking Instructions

1. Cut bell peppers in half lengthwise. Remove seeds and middle, leaving edges intact like bowls.
2. Apply a small amount of olive oil to the exposed edges.
3. Crack two eggs inside each bell pepper half and sprinkle with desired spices.
4. Place the bell peppers in your air fryer.
5. Set the air fryer to 390°F (200°C) for 13 minutes (adjust time for desired egg doneness).
6. For a less browned pepper, use one egg per half and set the air fryer to 330°F (165°C) for 15 minutes for an over-hard egg consistency.
7. Serve and enjoy your Stuffed Peppers!

Useful Tips

For extra flavor, add toppings such as shredded cheese, chopped herbs, or crumbled bacon to the eggs before cooking.

Allow the stuffed peppers to cool completely, then keep them in an airtight container in the refrigerator for up to 3 days.

Nutrition Facts for 1 Serving

Calories: 164 Kcal, Protein: 11 g, Fat: 2 g, Carbohydrates: 4 g, Sugar: 2 g, Cholesterol: 327 mg, Sodium: 146 mg.

TWICE-BAKED POTATOES

🕐 52 Min   🍽 8 Servings

Ingredients

- 4 russet potatoes
- 2 cups of shredded cheddar cheese
- 1 cup of chopped spinach
- 1/2 cup of diced ham*
- 1/4 cup of heavy cream
- 1 tablespoon of extra virgin olive oil
- 1 diced green bell pepper
- 2 diced Roma tomatoes
- 1/2 teaspoon of coarse black pepper
- 4 eggs
- 1 pinch of salt and pepper

Cooking Instructions

1. Preheat the air fryer to 400°F (205°C). Pierce potatoes, brush with olive oil, season with salt and pepper, and wrap in foil. Air fry for 40 minutes.
2. Cool for 15 minutes, slice in half, and scoop out insides. Mix the scooped potato with diced tomatoes, bell pepper, ham, spinach, eggs, 1 cup cheddar cheese, salt, and pepper.
3. Preheat the air fryer to 375°F (190°C). Fill potato shells with the mixture, top with remaining cheese, and air fry for 15 minutes.
4. Serve and enjoy your Twice-Baked Potatoes!

Useful Tips

*This recipe would also be excellent with crumbled cooked bacon instead of ham.
Store in the refrigerator. It will keep well for 3 days.

Nutrition Facts for 1 Serving

Calories: 301 Kcal, Protein: 15 g, Fat: 18 g, Carbohydrates: 22 g, Sugar: 3g, Cholesterol: 127 mg, Sodium: 620 mg, Sodium: 156 mg.

SPINACH & FETA OMELETTE

🕐 18 Min   🍽 1 Serving

Ingredients

- 1/3 cup of chopped spinach
- 1/3 cup of diced red bell pepper
- 1/4 cup of crumbled feta cheese
- 2 medium eggs
- Salt and black pepper, to taste

Cooking Instructions

1. Preheat your air fryer to 355°F (180°C) and prepare your air fryer liner or dish.
2. Whisk the eggs and add your desired mix-ins in a small bowl.
3. Pour the prepared egg mixture into the air fryer liner, ensuring it forms a single layer. Bake for 8-10 minutes, until fully cooked.
4. Carefully remove the liner from the air fryer, slice the frittata if desired, and enjoy! Remember, the liner will be hot immediately after cooking.
5. Serve and enjoy your Spinach & Feta Omelette!

Useful Tips

To simplify this recipe, prepare your ingredients the night before. In the morning, simply pour everything into the liner and place it in the air fryer.
Store in the refrigerator. It will keep well for 3 days.

Nutrition Facts for 1 Serving

Calories: 240 Kcal, Protein: 17 g, Fat: 17 g, Carbohydrates: 5 g, Sugar: 2 g, Cholesterol: 361 mg, Sodium: 562 mg.

AVOCADO TOAST WITH EGG

🕐 13 Min   🍴 2 Toasts

Ingredients

- 2 fried or poached eggs
- 1 large avocado*
- 2 pieces of bread
- 1 tablespoon of butter
- 1 teaspoon of salt
- 1/2 teaspoon of black pepper
- 1/2 teaspoon of red pepper flakes

Cooking Instructions

1. Place bread pieces inside the air fryer basket, set the temperature to 330°F (165°C), and air fry for 2 to 3 minutes.
2. In a small bowl, mash the avocado until creamy. Once the toast is cooked, spread the avocado over it.
3. Cook 2 eggs in a small saucepan. Heat the butter over low-medium heat, crack the egg into the skillet, and cook until set.
4. Place the cooked egg on top of the avocado toast and season with salt, crushed red pepper, and black pepper.
5. Serve and enjoy your Avocado Toast with Egg!

Useful Tips

* If you need to ripen your avocados quickly, place them in a brown paper bag. They will typically ripen in 1 to 2 days.
For better results, I recommend preparing and consuming avocado toast fresh, as the texture and flavor are best when freshly made.

Nutrition Facts for 1 Toast

Calories: 279 Kcal, Protein: 8 g, Fat: 2 g, Carbohydrates: 10 g, Sugar: 1 g, Cholesterol: 179 mg, Sodium: 1290 mg.

QUESADILLA

🕐 13 Min   🍴 4 Quesadillas

Ingredients

- 2 cups of shredded cheese
- 4 small to medium tortillas (flour or corn)
- 1 tablespoon of oil
- 1 teaspoon of taco seasoning
- 1 teaspoon of sliced green onions
- 1/2 chopped red bell pepper
- 1/2 chopped yellow or green bell pepper
- 1 small chopped onion
- 1/4 teaspoon of salt
- Non-aerosol non-stick spray

Cooking Instructions

1. Preheat your air fryer to 355°F (180°C). Wrap the vegetables in foil with oil, taco seasoning, and salt, then air fry for 5 minutes until softened.
2. Lightly grease the basket and place one tortilla inside. Layer with 1/4 cheese, half the veggies, half the green onions, and another 1/4 cheese. Top with the second tortilla and cook for 3-4 minutes per side.
3. Repeat for the second quesadilla. Remove and serve hot. Enjoy your Quesadilla!

Useful Tips

Ensure you flip your quesadilla halfway through cooking to achieve even crispiness on both sides. They can be kept in the refrigerator for up to 3 days.

Nutrition Facts for 1 Quesadilla

Calories: 134 Kcal, Protein: 6 g, Fat: 8 g, Carbohydrates: 10 g, Sugar: 2 g, Cholesterol: 17 mg, Sodium: 317 mg.

BREAKFAST BURRITOS

🕐 35 Min   🍴 6 Burritos

Ingredients

- 6 flour tortillas
- 1/2 pound of raw breakfast sausage
- 4 eggs
- 1 medium potato
- 1 cup of shredded cheddar cheese
- 1/4 cup of milk
- 1 tablespoon of oil
- 1 teaspoon of salt
- 1/2 teaspoon of ground black pepper

Cooking Instructions

1. Preheat your air fryer to 400°F.
2. Cut the peeled potato into 1/2" cubes and coat it with oil, pepper, and salt. Put in the preheated basket, fry at 400°F for 8 minutes, and set aside.
3. Fry the sausage in a skillet on medium heat. Remove it, leaving the grease inside the pan.
4. Whisk the milk, egg, a little pepper, and salt in a bowl. Pour it into a hot skillet with the grease. Scramble the eggs until fluffy.
5. Mix the potato, eggs, cheese, and the sausage in a bowl. Divide it between 6 tortillas and wrap them closed, using toothpicks.
6. Spray some oil over the burritos and transfer them into the basket. Fry them at 380°F for 7-8 minutes, flipping and adding oil halfway through cooking.
7. Serve warm with your favorite sauce!*

Useful Tips

* It tastes good with salsa, sour cream, or hot sauce.

Nutrition Facts for 1 Burrito

Calories: 484 Kcal, Protein: 22 g, Fat: 27 g, Carbohydrates: 37 g, Sugar: 1 g, Cholesterol: 179 mg.

EGG-BACON CUPS

🕐 20 Min   🍴 6 Servings

Ingredients

- 6 large eggs
- 3 slices of bacon
- 1/2 diced bell pepper
- Salt and ground black pepper, to taste

Cooking Instructions

1. Cut the bacon strips in half lengthwise. Place one half-slice of bacon on each silicone baking cup, ensuring it covers the surface of the cup.*
2. Gently crack an egg inside each cup, using the bacon as a base for the runny egg.
3. Sprinkle the tops with diced bell pepper, salt, and pepper to satisfy your taste buds.
4. Put the cups inside the air fryer basket. Carefully close the basket, ensuring that none of the cups topple over. Bake them at 330°F for about 10 minutes (the cooking time can vary based on how you like eggs). For getting over-medium eggs, you can start with 8 minutes; for over-well consistency, it will take 10 minutes. Remove the baked cups very carefully; they will be too hot.
5. Serve warm and enjoy Egg-Bacon Cups!

Useful Tips

* If you want to get crispier bacon, pre-cook bacon to medium-rare before lining it inside cups.
Keep the leftovers in an airtight food container in a fridge for up to 4 days.

Nutrition Facts for 1 Cup

Calories: 115 Kcal, Protein: 8 g, Carbohydrates: 0 g, Fat: 9 g, Sugar: 0 g, Cholesterol: 10 mg, Sodium: 160 mg.

GRILLED CHEESE SANDWICH

🕐 10 Min   🍴 1 Sandwich

Ingredients

- 2 slices of bread*
- 2 slices cheddar cheese
- 2 slices of turkey (optional)
- 1 teaspoon of butter

Cooking Instructions

1. Preheat your air fryer to 355°F (180°C).
2. Spread butter over one side of 2 bread slices. Layer cheese and turkey (if preferred) between the slices, ensuring the buttered sides face outwards.
3. Place the sandwich in the air fryer and cook for 5 minutes, flipping halfway through for even browning. Once golden and with the cheese nicely melted, your grilled cheese sandwich is ready to savor!
4. Serve and enjoy your Grilled Cheese Sandwich!

Useful Tips

* Sourdough bread is an excellent option for crafting the perfect crispy grilled cheese sandwich. Additionally, both white and whole-grain bread varieties offer delightful alternatives!

Store the wrapped sandwiches in the refrigerator for up to 2 days.

Nutrition Facts for 1 Sandwich

Calories: 455 Kcal, Protein: 26 g, Fat: 26 g, Carbohydrates: 28 g, Sugar: 3 g, Cholesterol: 91 mg, Sodium: 708 mg.

FLUFFY EGG BITES

🕐 18 Min   🍴 2 Servings

Ingredients

- 4 large eggs
- 1/4 cup of shredded cheese
- 2 tablespoons of diced ham
- 2 tablespoons of diced tomatoes
- 1 tablespoon of diced vegetables
- 1 tablespoon of milk*
- Cooking spray
- 1/2 teaspoon of salt and pepper to taste
- 1/2 teaspoon of seasoning of your choice

Cooking Instructions

1. Preheat your air fryer to 355°F (180°C).
2. Whisk together eggs and milk in a 2-cup measuring cup. Season with pepper, salt, and paprika. Stir in cheese, cooked bacon or sausage, and diced ham.
3. Pour the mixture into lightly greased silicone muffin cups or 4-oz ceramic ramekins. Place in the preheated air fryer basket and cook for 8-10 minutes until set and slightly golden.
4. Check for doneness, then use oven mitts or tongs to remove the cups. Run a knife around the edges and lift the egg bites with a spoon.
5. Serve and enjoy your Fluffy Egg Bites!

Useful Tips

*Instead of milk, you can add heavy cream or half and half.

Store in the refrigerator for up to 6 days.

Nutrition Facts for 1 Serving

Calories: 107 Kcal, Protein: 9 g, Fat: 7 g, Carbohydrates: 2 g, Sugar: 1 g, Cholesterol: 174 mg, Sodium: 487 mg.

CHICKEN PARMESAN

🕐 50 Min   🍴 4 Servings

Ingredients

- 2 large skinless, boneless chicken breasts
- 2 large eggs
- 1/3 cup of all-purpose flour
- 1 cup of panko breadcrumbs
- 1/4 cup of freshly grated Parmesan
- 1/2 teaspoon of crushed red pepper flakes
- 1 teaspoon of dried oregano
- 1/2 teaspoon of garlic powder
- 1 cup of marinara
- 1 cup of shredded mozzarella
- Kosher salt
- Freshly ground black pepper
- Freshly chopped parsley, for garnish

Cooking Instructions

1. Cut chicken in half widthwise to create 4 thin pieces, season with salt and pepper. Coat in flour, then eggs, and finally a panko mixture (oregano, red pepper flakes, Parmesan, panko, garlic powder).
2. Air fry at 400°F (205°C) for 5 minutes per side, top with marinara and mozzarella, and cook for 3 more minutes until the cheese melts. Serve warm, garnished with parsley.
3. Enjoy your Chicken Parmesan!

Useful Tips

Store in the refrigerator for up to 3-4 days.

Nutrition Facts for 1 Serving

Calories: 120 Kcal, Protein: 11 g, Fat: 4 g, Carbohydrates: 8 g, Sugar: 1 g, Cholesterol: 63 mg, Sodium: 283 mg.

TERIYAKI CHICKEN

🕐 30 Min   🍴 4 Servings

Ingredients

- 1/2 pound of broccoli, cut into pieces
- 1 pound of cubed chicken, boneless chicken breasts, or thighs
- 1/4 cup of teriyaki sauce
- 1/4 teaspoon of salt
- 1/4 teaspoon of pepper
- cooking spray
- sesame seeds
- soy sauce (optional)

Cooking Instructions

1. Cut chicken and broccoli into bite-sized pieces. Preheat the air fryer to 355°F (180°C).
2. Place chicken and broccoli in the air fryer basket, spritz with cooking spray, and season with salt and pepper. Air fry for 15 minutes, then coat with teriyaki sauce and air fry for another 5 minutes. Check that the chicken reaches an internal temperature of 165°F (75°C).
3. Sprinkle with sesame seeds and serve with soy sauce*. Enjoy your Teriyaki Chicken & Broccoli!

Useful Tips

* Serve the air-fried teriyaki chicken and broccoli with soy sauce on the side for dipping, noodles or alongside steamed rice for a complete meal. Store in the refrigerator for up to 3-4 days.

Nutrition Facts for 1 Serving

Calories: 326 Kcal, Protein: 31 g, Fat: 19 g, Carbohydrates: 9 g, Sugar: 3 g, Cholesterol: 107 mg, Sodium: 927 mg.

ORANGE CHICKEN

🕐 40 Min   🍴 4-6 Servings

Ingredients

- 2 pounds of skinless, boneless chicken breasts
- 2 large eggs
- 1 1/2 cups of orange juice
- 1/4 cup of all-purpose flour
- 1/4 cup of light brown sugar
- 2 minced garlic cloves garlic
- 1/2 cup of plus 1 tablespoon cornstarch
- 2 tablespoons of tamari or low-sodium soy sauce
- 2 tablespoons of rice vinegar
- 2 teaspoons of toasted sesame oil
- 1/2 teaspoon of kosher salt
- 1/2 teaspoon of minced fresh ginger
- 1/4 teaspoon of ground black pepper
- 1/4 teaspoon of crushed red pepper flakes

Cooking Instructions

1. Pat chicken dry, season with salt and pepper, then coat in beaten eggs and a mixture of cornstarch and flour. Air fry at 400°F (205°C) for 10 minutes, tossing and spraying with cooking spray halfway through.
2. In a pot, cook garlic, red pepper flakes, and ginger until fragrant. Add a mixture of brown sugar, orange juice, vinegar, soy sauce, and cornstarch, then simmer until thickened. Pour over cooked chicken, toss to coat.
3. Serve warm and enjoy your Orange Chicken!

Useful Tips

Leftover portions can be stored for 4 days.

Nutrition Facts for 1 Serving

Calories: 60 Kcal, Protein: 6 g, Fat: 1 g, Carbohydrates: 7 g, Sugar: 4 g, Cholesterol: 10 mg, Sodium: 50 mg.

DUCK PANCAKES

🕐 1 Hour   🍴 4 Pancakes

Ingredients

- 4-5 pounds of whole duck
- 8 Chinese pancakes
- 1 lime
- 1 cucumber
- 2 teaspoons of Chinese five-spice
- 2 ounces of spring onions
- Hoisin sauce

Cooking Instructions

1. Season the duck with Chinese five-spice and insert half a lime into its cavity. Place it in the air fryer and cook at 355°F (180°C) for 1 hour.
2. After 20 minutes of cooking, carefully drain some of the oil from the air fryer basket into a bowl to discard later. Lightly brush the duck with some of the oil, avoiding excessive coating.
3. Once cooked, let the duck rest for 15 minutes. Then, carve the meat from the bone using a knife and shred it roughly using two forks.
4. While the duck is resting, steam the Chinese pancakes (you can use a microwave for this), slice the spring onions lengthwise, and cut the cucumber into thin matchsticks.
5. Serve the pancakes with the shredded duck, sliced spring onions, cucumber matchsticks, and hoisin sauce.
6. Serve and enjoy your Duck Pancakes!

Useful Tips

Store the duck in the fridge for 4 days.

Nutrition Facts for 1 Pancake

Calories: 565 Kcal, Protein: 6 g, Fat: 4 g, Carbohydrates: 6 g, Sugar: 1 g, Cholesterol: 56 mg, Sodium: 112 mg.

SESAME CHICKEN THIGHS

⏱ 55 Min   🍴 4 Servings

Ingredients

- 2 tablespoons of sesame oil
- 2 tablespoons of soy sauce
- 1 tablespoon of honey
- 1 tablespoon of sriracha sauce
- 1 teaspoon of rice vinegar
- 2 pounds of chicken thighs
- 1 chopped green onion
- 2 tablespoons of toasted sesame seeds

Cooking Instructions

1. Mix together honey, sesame oil, vinegar, soy sauce, and sriracha in a spacious bowl. Add the chicken, ensuring it's coated well. Cover and keep in a refrigerate for at least 30 minutes.
2. Preheat the air fryer to 400°F (205°C). Remove the refrigerated chicken from the marinade and drain any excess.
3. Arrange the chicken thighs skin-side up in the air fryer basket. Cook for about 5 minutes, then flip on the other side and cook for an additional 10 minutes*.
4. Once cooked, transfer the chicken to a serving plate and let it rest for 5 minutes. Sprinkle over with toasted sesame seeds and chopped green onions as garnish.
5. Serve and enjoy your Sesame Chicken Thighs!

Useful Tips

Store in a fridge for up to 3-4 days.

Nutrition Facts for 1 Serving

Calories: 121 Kcal, Protein: 10 g, Fat: 8 g, Carbohydrates: 2 g, Sugar: 1 g, Cholesterol: 43 mg, Sodium: 185 m.

WHOLE CHICKEN

⏱ 1 Hour 25 Min   🍴 8 Servings

Ingredients

- 2 tablespoons of olive oil
- 2 1/2 teaspoons of Italian seasoning
- 2 1/2 teaspoons of poultry seasoning
- 2 teaspoons of paprika
- 2 teaspoons of salt
- 1 (5 pounds) whole chicken, giblets removed

Cooking Instructions

1. Preheat the air fryer to 355°F (180°C).
2. In a small bowl, mix Italian seasoning, olive oil, paprika, poultry seasoning, and salt until well combined.
3. Use paper towels to pat the chicken dry. Brush the spice mixture evenly over the entire chicken, ensuring it covers even underneath the wings.
4. Position the chicken in the air fryer basket with the breast side facing down. Cook undisturbed for 45 minutes. Carefully flip the chicken using tongs and continue cooking until it reaches an internal temperature of 165°F (75°C), approximately 20 minutes longer*.
5. Transfer the cooked chicken to a cutting board and allow it to rest for 10 minutes before serving.
6. Serve warm and enjoy your Whole Chicken!

Useful Tips

* Use a meat thermometer to check the internal temperature of the chicken. It should reach an internal temperature of 165°F (75°C) to ensure they are fully cooked. Store in a fridge for up to 4 days.

Nutrition Facts for 1 Serving

Calories: 34 Kcal, Protein: 3 g, Fat: 4 g, Carbohydrates: 1 g, Sugar: 0 g, Cholesterol: 35 mg, Sodium: 122 mg.

CITRUS & HERB TURKEY

🕐 35 Min   🍴 4 Servings

Ingredients

- 1 turkey half-breast with rib meat (2.5 pounds)
- 4 teaspoons of kosher salt
- 4 teaspoons of olive oil
- 2 teaspoons of orange zest, finely grated
- 2 teaspoons of fresh thyme leaves
- 2 teaspoons of roughly chopped rosemary leaves
- 1 teaspoon of dark brown sugar
- 1 teaspoon of aniseed or fennel seed
- 1/2 teaspoon of ground black pepper

Cooking Instructions

1. Toast aniseed or fennel seed in a dry skillet for 2 minutes, then cool and grind. In a food processor, combine brown sugar, salt, orange zest, thyme, rosemary, ground aniseed or fennel seed, and pepper, pulsing until finely chopped.
2. Rub the herb mixture on the turkey breast and refrigerate uncovered for 4-6 hours. Rinse, pat dry, and coat with olive oil. Preheat the air fryer to 330°F (165°C).
3. Bake the turkey breast skin-side up in the air fryer for 40 minutes. Let it rest for 10 minutes before slicing.
4. Serve warm and enjoy Citrus & Herb Turkey!

Useful Tips

Use a meat thermometer to check the internal temperature of the turkey. It should reach an internal temperature of 165°F (75°C) to ensure they are fully cooked. Store in a fridge for up to 4 days.

Nutrition Facts for 1 Serving

Calories: 56 Kcal, Protein: 6 g, Fat: 3 g, Carbohydrates: 1 g, Sugar: 1 g, Cholesterol: 18 mg, Sodium: 450 mg.

CHICKEN LOLLIPOP

🕐 25 Min   🍴 8 Lollipops

Ingredients

- 6 drumsticks
- 1 cup of BBQ sauce
- 1 tablespoon of honey

Cooking Instructions

1. Take each chicken drumstick and create incisions around the base of the bone, aiming to cut through the tendons and skin without touching the bone itself. Grasp the bone end of the drumstick and push the meat downwards to shape it into a lollipop form. This may require some pressure, so continue pushing until the meat forms a rounded shape at the bottom. Repeat this process for all drumsticks.
2. Next, combine honey and BBQ sauce to create the marinade mixture. Coat each chicken piece thoroughly with the marinade and place it in the air fryer. Wrap any exposed bone with foil to prevent burning.
3. Cook the drumsticks in the air fryer at 400°F (205°C) for 15 minutes. Midway through the cooking process, baste the drumsticks with additional marinade for added flavor.
4. Serve warm and enjoy your Chicken Lollipop!

Useful Tips

Pat chicken legs dry with a clean towel before marinating for extra crispy skin.

Keep it cooked in the container in the refrigerator for up to 4 days.

Nutrition Facts for 1 Lollipop

Calories: 259 Kcal, Protein: 22 g, Fat: 8 g, Carbohydrates: 22g, Sugar: 19g, Cholesterol: 116mg, Sodium: 573 mg.

POPCORN CHICKEN

🕐 40 Min   🍴 4 Servings

Ingredients

- 1 tablespoon of olive oil
- 1 1/2 cup of panko breadcrumbs
- 1 teaspoon of kosher salt
- 1 pound of boneless, skinless chicken breasts
- 2 tablespoons of all-purpose flour
- 1 large egg
- 2 teaspoons of garlic powder
- 2 teaspoons of onion powder
- 1 teaspoon of dried oregano
- 1/8 teaspoon of cayenne pepper, optional
- Freshly ground black pepper

Cooking Instructions

1. Heat a skillet with some oil on medium-low heat. Toast panko with salt until golden, about 4 minutes. Transfer to a plate. Cut chicken into cubes, season, and set up the dredging station.
2. For the dredging station: flour and salt on a plate, egg beaten with water in a bowl, and panko mixed with seasonings on another plate.
3. Dredge chicken in flour and egg, then panko mixture. Spray the basket with oil and preheat the air fryer to 400°F (205°C). Cook chicken in batches for 5 minutes, shaking halfway.
4. Serve hot and enjoy your Popcorn Chicken!

Useful Tips

Store cooked in a fridge for up to 4 days.

Nutrition Facts for 1 Serving (15 pieces)

Calories: 283 Kcal, Protein: 30 g, Fat: 8 g, Carbohydrates: 21 g, Sugar: 2 g, Cholesterol: 129 mg, Sodium: 385 mg.

BBQ DUCK BREAST

🕐 40 Min   🍴 1 Duck Breast

Ingredients

- 1 duck breast
- 3 tablespoons of soy sauce
- 2 1/2 tablespoons of lee kum kee oyster sauce
- 2 tablespoons of honey
- 1 1/2 tablespoons of minced garlic
- 1 tablespoon of five-spice powder

Cooking Instructions

1. Dry the duck breast thoroughly, especially the skin. Combine oyster sauce, soy sauce, five-spice powder, minced garlic, and honey. Place the duck breast in the marinade, ensuring the skin doesn't touch the sauce. Let it marinate in the refrigerator overnight, leaving some space for air circulation (poke holes in the plastic wrap if necessary).
2. Place the duck in the air fryer with the skin side facing up, patting the skin dry once more. Cook at 300°F (150°C) for 15 minutes.
3. In a separate bowl, mix honey, warm water, and five-spice powder. After 15 minutes, brush the honey mixture over the duck breast and fry at 400°F (205°C) for 10 minutes or until crispy and golden brown.
4. Serve hot and enjoy your BBQ Duck Breast!

Useful Tips

You can marinate the duck breast and refrigerate it for a maximum of 2 days.
Store cooked in a fridge for up to 4 days.

Nutrition Facts for 1 Duck Breast

Calories: 502 Kcal, Protein: 53 g, Fat: 11 g, Carbohydrates: 50g, Cholesterol: 174 mg, Sugar: 2g, Sodium: 4379 mg.

SPICY DUCK LEG

🕐 45 Min   🍴 4 Servings

Ingredients

- 2 duck legs
- 4 tablespoons of olive oil
- Juice of 1 orange
- 1 teaspoon of granulated garlic
- 1/2 teaspoon of fresh ginger
- Chili powder, as much as you like
- 1/2 teaspoon of kosher salt
- 1/2 teaspoon of black pepper

Cooking Instructions

1. Combine all marinade ingredients.
2. Thoroughly coat the duck legs with the marinade. Place them in an airtight container and refrigerate for at least 2-4 hours to marinate.
3. Set the air fryer at 355°F (180°C) and cook for 25 minutes*.
4. Turn the duck legs every 7-10 minutes to ensure even cooking.
5. Serve warm and enjoy your Spicy Duck Legs with a side of salad and grilled potatoes!

Useful Tips

* Halfway through cooking, check the duck leg. If it appears very pink and juicy, lower the temperature to 340°F (170°C) and extend the air frying time by 10 minutes.
Store cooked in a fridge for up to 4 days.

Nutrition Facts for 1 Serving

Calories: 405 Kcal, Protein: 20 g, Fat: 37 g, Carbohydrates: 2 g, Sugar: 2 g, Cholesterol: 87 mg, Sodium: 323 mg.

GROUND TURKEY MEATBALLS

🕐 30 Min   🍴 20 Meatballs

Ingredients

- 1 pound of fat-free ground turkey breast
- 1 cup of coarsely chopped zucchini
- 1/4 cup of grated Pecorino Romano cheese
- 1/2 cup of coarsely chopped onion
- 1/4 cup of chopped fresh parsley
- 1/3 cup of panko breadcrumbs
- 1 large egg
- 1/2 teaspoon of kosher salt
- 1/2 teaspoon of black pepper
- 1 chopped garlic clove

Cooking Instructions

1. Blend garlic, zucchini, onion, and parsley in a food processor. Transfer to a bowl, then add salt, panko, cheese, egg, pepper and turkey. Mix well* and shape into 20 meatballs.
2. Preheat the air fryer to 400°F (205°C). Lightly coat the basket with nonstick spray. Cook 10 meatballs for 5 minutes, then remove (they'll be partially cooked). Repeat with the remaining meatballs.
3. Return all meatballs to the basket and air-fry for extra 5 minutes until fully cooked.
4. Serve warm and enjoy your Ground Turkey Meatballs!

Useful Tips

*Ensure the mixture is well-combined, but avoid overmixing to maintain a tender texture.
Store cooked in a fridge for up to 4 days.

Nutrition Facts for 5 Meatballs

Calories: 170 Kcal, Protein: 22 g, Fat: 6 g, Carbohydrates: 4 g, Sugar: 1 g, Cholesterol: 118 mg, Sodium: 224 mg.

CHICKEN WINGS

⏱ 45 Min   🍽 4 Servings

Ingredients

- 2 pounds of chicken wings
- 1/4 cup of hot sauce
- 4 tablespoons of melted butter
- 1 teaspoon of Worcestershire sauce
- Kosher salt and freshly ground black pepper
- Blue cheese dressing, for serving

Cooking Instructions

1. Season wings with salt and pepper. Spray the air fryer with nonstick cooking spray.
2. Cook wings at 380°F (195°C) for 12 minutes, flip, and cook for another 12 minutes. Increase heat to 400°F (205°C) and cook for an additional 5 minutes.
3. In a large bowl, whisk together hot sauce, Worcestershire sauce, melted butter, and garlic powder. Toss cooked wings in the sauce.
4. Serve with blue cheese dressing.
5. Enjoy your Chicken Wings!

Useful Tips

Dry the chicken with paper towels before marinating for extra crispy skin.
Store cooked in a fridge for up to 4 days.

Nutrition Facts for 1 Serving

Calories: 606 Kcal, Protein: 40 g, Fat: 48 g, Carbohydrates: 2 g, Sugar: 1 g, Cholesterol: 285 mg, Sodium: 629 mg.

CHICKEN SATAY

⏱ 55 Min   🍽 8 Satays

Ingredients

- 1 pound of chicken thigh fillets, diced into ¾-inch pieces
- 1 crushed garlic clove
- 1 teaspoon of finely grated fresh ginger
- 1 teaspoon of brown sugar
- 1/2 teaspoon of ground turmeric
- 1 tablespoon of vegetable oil
- 1 teaspoon of soy sauce
- Finely grated rind of 1 lime
- 1/4 cup of coconut milk
- 1 tablespoon of fresh lime juice
- 1 tablespoon of kecap manis
- 1/3 cup of natural peanut butter

Cooking Instructions

1. Mix sugar, lime rind, ginger, turmeric, garlic, oil, and soy sauce in a dish. Coat chicken and refrigerate for 1-8 hours.
2. Blend coconut milk, peanut butter, kecap manis, chili, and lime juice. Add water and stir until smooth.
3. Skewer the marinated chicken and grease the air fryer basket. Air fry the skewers at 355°F (180°C) for 5 minutes, flip, and cook for another 5 minutes. Repeat with the remaining skewers.
4. Serve and enjoy the Chicken Satay!

Useful Tips

Store cooked in a fridge for up to 4 days.

Nutrition Facts for 1 Satay

Calories: 244 Kcal, Protein: 13 g, Fat: 19 g, Carbohydrates: 5 g, Sugar: 2 g, Cholesterol: 56 mg, Sodium: 132 mg.

ROASTED TURKEY LEGS

🕐 45 Min   🍽 2 Servings

Ingredients

- 2 large turkey legs
- 1 1/2 teaspoons of smoked paprika
- 1 teaspoon of seasoned salt
- 1 teaspoon of brown sugar
- 1/2 teaspoon of garlic powder

Cooking Instructions

1. Mix the smoked paprika, garlic powder, seasoned salt, and brown sugar in a bowl.
2. Wash and dry the turkey legs with a paper towel. Rub them with the seasoning mixture to coat evenly.
3. Put the turkey inside the air fryer basket and lightly spray over with olive oil.
4. Roast it at 400°F for 20 minutes, flip the turkey legs, and continue cooking for 20 minutes more.
5. Serve warm and enjoy your Roasted Turkey Legs!

Useful Tips

You can keep the leftovers in the refrigerator for up to 4 days. Just reheat them at 360°F for 5 minutes before serving.

Nutrition Facts for 1 Serving

Calories: 988 Kcal, Protein: 133 g, Fat: 46 g, Carbohydrates: 3 g, Sugar: 2 g, Cholesterol: 197 mg.

ALMOND CRUSTED CHICKEN

🕐 15 Min   🍽 4 Servings

Ingredients

- 2 large skinless and boneless chicken breasts
- 1/2 cup of chopped almonds
- 1/4 cup of mayonnaise
- 2 tablespoons of Dijon mustard
- 1/4 teaspoon of salt
- 1/4 teaspoon of ground black pepper

Cooking Instructions

1. Preheat your air fryer to 375°F. Spray some oil inside the basket.
2. Slice each chicken breast horizontally, making two thin cutlets to cook them evenly. Sprinkle with pepper and salt.
3. Mix the Dijon mustard and mayonnaise in a small bowl. Spread it over one side of each chicken piece.
4. Chop the almonds finely using a food processor. Pulse for 8-10 times. Avoid turning to flour. Spread it over the mayo-mustard chicken side, pressing down.
5. Place the chicken inside the basket, laying the almond-crusted side down. Brush the other side with the mayo-mustard mixture and spoon it with the almonds. Air fry it at 375°F for 9 minutes until the internal temperature reaches 165°F. Serve warm and enjoy it!

Useful Tips

You can keep the leftovers in an airtight food container in a fridge for up to 3 days. Just reheat at 350°F for 3-4 minutes before serving.

Nutrition Facts for 1 Serving

Calories: 185 Kcal, Protein: 16 g, Fat: 11 g, Carbohydrates: 7 g, Sugar: 2 g, Cholesterol: 37 mg.

BACON & CHICKEN BITES

🕐 35 Min   🍴 12 Bites

Ingredients

- 2 boneless, skinless chicken breasts, cut into even bite-size strips (approximately 1" thick and 2-3" in length) or chicken tenderloins
- 6 slices of regular thin-cut bacon
- 1 tablespoon of olive oil
- 1/2 teaspoon of salt and pepper
- 1/2 teaspoon of garlic powder
- 1/4 teaspoon of smoked paprika
- 1/4 teaspoon of onion powder
- 1 tablespoon of chopped parsley, optionally

Cooking Instructions

1. Combine chicken strips with oil and spices in a bowl, mixing until fully coated. Cover and refrigerate for 20-30 minutes.
2. Preheat air fryer to 400°F (205°C) or run empty for 3 minutes. Wrap each chicken strip with half a piece of bacon, securing it with toothpicks if needed.
3. Place bacon-wrapped chicken in the air fryer basket without overlapping. Air fry at 400°F (205°C) for 10-12 minutes, flipping halfway, until the bacon is crispy, and the chicken reaches 165°F (75°C).
4. Serve and enjoy your Bacon & Chicken Bites.

Useful Tips

For added flavor, marinate the chicken for a few hours before seasoning and wrapping it in bacon. Store cooked in a fridge for up to 4 days.

Nutrition Facts for 1 Bite

Calories: 73 Kcal, Protein: 9 g, Fat: 4 g, Carbohydrates: 0 g, Sugar: 0 g, Cholesterol: 28 mg, Sodium: 208 mg.

TURKEY MEATLOAF

🕐 37 Min   🍴 4 Servings

Ingredients

- 1 pound of ground turkey
- 1 small finely diced onion
- 2 finely minced garlic cloves
- 1/4 cup of ketchup*
- 10 crushed crackers
- 1 egg
- 1 tablespoon of brown sugar
- 1 teaspoon of salt, or to taste
- 1 teaspoon of Italian seasoning
- 1 teaspoon of Worcestershire sauce
- 1/4 teaspoon of black pepper
- 1/2 teaspoon of granulated garlic
- Pinch of crushed red pepper

Cooking Instructions

1. In a large bowl, mix all ingredients except ketchup and sugar. Shape into a loaf on a baking sheet.
2. Preheat the air fryer to 355°F (180°C). Place the meatloaf in the greased basket and cook for 20 minutes.
3. Mix ketchup and brown sugar. After 20 minutes, brush the mixture over the meatloaf and cook for an extra 7 minutes.
4. Let the meatloaf rest for 10 minutes before slicing. Serve and enjoy your Turkey Meatloaf!

Useful Tips

If you're not a fan of ketchup, use BBQ sauce instead. Store cooked in a fridge for up to 4 days.

Nutrition Facts for 1 Serving

Calories: 55 Kcal, Protein: 7 g, Fat: 2 g, Carbohydrates: 4 g, Sugar: 2 g, Cholesterol: 26 mg.

CRISPY CHICKEN NUGGETS

🕐 18 Min   🍴 4 Servings

Ingredients

- 1 boneless, skinless chicken breast
- 1/2 cup of melted unsalted butter
- 1/2 cup of breadcrumbs
- 2 tablespoons of grated Parmesan (optional)
- 1/4 teaspoon of salt
- 1/8 teaspoon of black pepper

Cooking Instructions

1. Preheat the air fryer to 390°F (200°C) for 4 minutes. Cut the chicken into nugget-sized pieces, season with salt and pepper.
2. Dip in melted butter, then coat with breadcrumbs (and Parmesan if using). Arrange in a single layer in the air fryer basket.
3. Cook for 8 minutes until nuggets reach 165°F (75°C). Let cool and serve.
4. Enjoy your Crispy Chicken Nuggets!

Useful Tips

Serve it with roasted or steamed vegetables or fruit salad and yogurt.
Store the cooked chicken nuggets in the fridge for up to 3 days.

Nutrition Facts for 1 Serving

Calories: 337 Kcal, Protein: 16 g, Fat: 25 g, Carbohydrates: 10 g, Cholesterol: 100 mg, Sugar: 1g, Sodium: 327 mg.

BREADED DRUMSTICKS

🕐 55 Min   🍴 4 Servings

Ingredients

- 3 pounds of chicken drumsticks
- 1 cup of panko breadcrumbs
- 1/4 cup of buttermilk
- 2 teaspoons of chicken seasoning
- Salt and pepper to taste
- Cooking oil spray

Cooking Instructions

1. Drizzle chicken with buttermilk and refrigerate for 30 minutes.
2. Spray the air fryer basket with cooking oil. Mix panko breadcrumbs with chicken seasoning, salt, and pepper. Coat chicken in panko mixture and spray both sides with cooking oil.
3. Air fry at 380°F (195°C) for 10 minutes. Flip and cook for another 10-14 minutes until the internal temperature reaches 165°F (75°C). Reduce heat to 355°F (180°C) if browning too quickly.
4. Let cool before serving. Enjoy your Breaded Drumsticks!

Useful Tips

Buttermilk is commonly used in fried chicken recipes to brine the chicken and create a crunchy crust. If you need a substitute, try using eggs instead.
Store the cooked chicken drumsticks in the fridge for up to 3 days.

Nutrition Facts for 1 Serving

Calories: 466 Kcal, Protein: 56 g, Fat: 18 g, Carbohydrates: 20 g, Sugar: 1 g, Cholesterol: 112 mg, Sodium: 452 mg

CHICKEN QUESADILLAS

⏱ 20 Min   🍴 8 Quesadillas

Ingredients

- 2 cups of shredded cooked chicken
- 2 cups of grated cheese*
- 8 (8-inch) flour tortillas
- 1 teaspoon of chili powder
- 1 teaspoon of ground cumin
- 1/4 teaspoon of cayenne pepper
- 16 wooden toothpicks
- Olive oil cooking spray

Cooking Instructions

1. Preheat the air fryer to 355°F (180°C). Toss chicken with chili powder, cumin, and cayenne pepper.
2. Lay a tortilla flat, sprinkle 2 tablespoons of cheese over half, add the chicken mixture, then sprinkle another 2 tablespoons of cheese. Fold in half and secure with wooden picks. Spray both sides with olive oil cooking spray.
3. Air fry quesadillas in a single layer for about 4 minutes per side until the cheese is melted and the tortillas are lightly browned. Cook in batches if needed.
4. Serve warm with your favorite toppings. Enjoy your Chicken Quesadillas!

Useful Tips

* Use a blend of cheeses that melt easily, such as Monterey Jack, Cheddar, or Pepper Jack.
Store any leftovers in the fridge for up to 2 days.

Nutrition Facts for 1 Quesadilla

Calories: 311 Kcal, Protein: 18 g, Fat: 15 g, Carbohydrates: 25 g, Sugar: 0 g, Cholesterol: 53 mg, Sodium: 423 mg.

TURKEY BURGER

⏱ 20 Min   🍴 4 Burgers

Ingredients

- 1 pound of 93% lean ground turkey*
- 1/3 cup of shredded yellow onion
- 3 tablespoons of finely chopped fresh parsley
- 2 teaspoons of Dijon mustard
- 2 large, minced garlic cloves
- 1 teaspoon of onion powder
- 1 teaspoon of salt
- 1/2 teaspoon of black pepper
- 1 teaspoon of dried Italian seasoning (optional)
- 4 buns or lettuce to serve

Cooking Instructions

1. Preheat the air fryer to 355°F (180°C).
2. In a bowl, mix ground turkey, shredded onion, Dijon mustard, minced garlic, parsley, onion powder, Italian seasoning, salt, and pepper. Shape into four 1/2-inch thick patties.
3. Air fry for 10-13 minutes, flipping halfway, until cooked through. Add cheese at the last minute if desired.
4. Assemble burgers with buns, lettuce wraps, or on a salad. Add toppings like red onion, lettuce, tomato, and cheddar cheese.
5. Serve and enjoy your delicious Turkey Burger!

Useful Tips

* Opt for 93% lean ground turkey to ensure juicier burgers.
Store cooked burgers in the refrigerator for 4-5 days.

Nutrition Facts for 1 Burger

Calories: 184 Kcal, Protein: 22 g, Fat: 10 g, Carbohydrates: 3 g, Sugar: 0 g, Cholesterol: 84 mg, Sodium: 690 mg.

DELICIOUS RIBEYE STEAK

🕐 45 Min   🍴 2 Servings

Ingredients

- 1 (2 pounds) bone-in ribeye
- 4 tablespoons of softened butter
- 2 minced garlic cloves
- 2 teaspoons of freshly chopped parsley
- 1 teaspoon of freshly chopped chives
- 1 teaspoon of freshly chopped thyme
- 1 teaspoon of freshly chopped rosemary
- Kosher salt and ground black pepper

Cooking Instructions

1. Mix the butter, garlic, and herbs in a small bowl. Transfer the mixture to the center of a piece of plastic wrap, shape it into a log, and twist the ends to seal. Refrigerate until firm, about 20 minutes.
2. Season the steak with pepper and salt.
3. Place the meat inside the basket and cook at 400°F (205°C) for 12 to 14 minutes for medium doneness*, flipping halfway through, depending on the thickness of the steak.
4. Serve the steak topped with a slice of herb butter and enjoy your Delicious Ribeye Steak!

Useful Tips

Use a meat thermometer to check steak temperature: Rare 125°F (55°C), Medium-rare 135°F (60°C), Medium 145°F (65°C).
Store in the refrigerator for 4 days.

Nutrition Facts for 1 Serving

Calories: 2455 Kcal, Protein: 141 g, Fat: 210 g, Carbohydrates: 3 g, Sugar: 0 g, Cholesterol: 668 mg, Sodium: 2274 mg.

CRISPY CHILI BEEF

🕐 25 Min   🍴 2 Servings

Ingredients

- 1 pound of flank steak, thinly sliced
- 2 tablespoons of soy sauce
- 1 tablespoon cornstarch
- 1 red bell pepper, thinly sliced
- 1 green bell pepper, thinly sliced
- 2 garlic cloves, minced
- 1 tablespoon chili paste*
- Salt and pepper to taste

Cooking Instructions

1. Marinate the Beef: Toss the steak with soy sauce and cornstarch.
2. Preheat the air fryer to 400°F (200°C). Cook beef for 8-10 minutes, shaking halfway through.
3. Prepare the Sauce: Sauté garlic and bell peppers for 2 minutes. Add chili paste and cook for another 2 minutes.
4. Combine and Serve: Mix beef with the sauce and vegetables. Season with salt and pepper.
5. Serve and enjoy your Crispy Chili Beef!

Useful Tips

* Adjust chili paste for spiciness.
Store leftovers in the refrigerator for up to 4 days.

Nutrition Facts for 1 Serving

Calories: 550 Kcal, Protein: 40 g, Fat: 25 g, Carbohydrates: 15 g, Sugar: 5 g, Cholesterol: 80 mg, Sodium: 900 mg.

NACHO CHEESE MEATBALLS

🕐 20 Min 🍽 16 Meatballs

Ingredients

- 1 pound of 96% lean ground beef
- 2 cups of crushed nacho cheese-flavored tortilla chips
- 1 can (4 ounces) of chopped mild green chilies, drained
- 16 cubes of pepper jack or Colby jack cheese (1/2 inch squares)
- 2 tablespoons of taco seasoning
  1 egg white
- 1 tablespoon of water
- 6 tablespoons of prepared thick taco sauce
- 3 tablespoons of honey

Cooking Instructions

1. Mix taco seasoning, green chilies, and ground beef in a bowl. Divide into 16 portions, shape around cheese cubes, and coat with egg white and crushed chips.
2. Arrange on an air fryer tray, and cook at 400°F (205°C) for 14 minutes, flipping halfway, until internal temperature reaches 160°F. Warm the sauce in the microwave for 30 seconds.
3. Serve and enjoy your Nacho Cheese Meatballs!

Useful Tips

To ensure all meatballs are the same size and cook evenly, use a spoon, cookie scoop, or measuring spoon to portion the beef.
Store any leftovers in an airtight container in the refrigerator for up to 3 days.

Nutrition Facts for 1 Serving

Calories: 499 Kcal, Protein: 34 g, Fat: 24 g, Carbohydrates: 37g, Cholesterol: 110mg, Sugar: 15g, Sodium: 1062 mg.

BEEF JERKY

🕐 2 Hours 15 Min 🍽 10 Servings

Ingredients

- 1 pound of thinly sliced beef steak (sirloin steak, round steak)
- 1 tablespoon of honey
- 1/2 teaspoon of chili flakes (optional)
- 1 teaspoon of onion powder
- 1/2 cup of soy sauce
- 1/2 cup of Worcestershire sauce

Cooking Instructions

1. Combine all marinade ingredients in a bowl.
2. Cut the beef slices into strips or squares and add them to the marinade, ensuring all surfaces are covered.
3. Cover the bowl and refrigerate for at least 3 hours or overnight.
4. Remove the beef from the marinade and pat dry with paper towels.
5. Place the beef strips in a single layer in the air fryer basket, ensuring they do not overlap.
6. Air fry at 175°F (80°C) for two hours. Check the jerky; if it's not fully dehydrated, continue air frying in 15-20-minute intervals until completely dried, reaching 160°F (75°C).
7. Serve and enjoy your Beef Jerky!

Useful Tips

Beef should be no thicker than 1/4 inch thick. Partially freezing the beef can make it easier to slice. For longer storage, keep the beef jerky in the refrigerator. It can last up to 2 weeks in the fridge.

Nutrition Facts for 1 Serving

Calories: 93 Kcal, Protein: 8 g, Fat: 6 g, Carbohydrates: 3 g, Sugar: 2 g, Cholesterol: 11 mg, Sodium: 472 mg.

34

BEEF JOINT

🕐 50 Min   🍴 8 Servings

Ingredients

- 2 3/4 pounds of beef roasting joint
- 1-2 tablespoons of neutral-flavored oil
- 1 teaspoon of dried thyme
- 1 teaspoon of onion granules
- 1 teaspoon of mustard powder

Cooking Instructions

1. Take the beef from the fridge and let it come to room temperature for 20-30 minutes before cooking.
2. Preheat the air fryer to 430°F (220°C). Rub the beef with oil. In a bowl, mix thyme, onion granules, mustard powder, 1 tsp salt, and 1 tsp ground black pepper. Rub this mixture all over the beef joint. Place the beef in the air fryer basket and cook for 10 minutes.
3. Reduce the temperature to 340°F (170°C) and cook for an additional 30-40 minutes (30 minutes for medium-rare, 40 minutes for medium-well). Transfer the meat to a board, cover loosely with foil, and let it rest for up to 30 minutes before carving and serving.
4. Serve and enjoy your Beef Joint!

Useful Tips

To achieve your desired level of doneness, use a meat thermometer to check the internal temperature. Store the wrapped beef joint or slices in the refrigerator. It will keep well for up to 3-4 days.

Nutrition Facts for 1 Serving

Calories: 255 Kcal, Protein: 31 g, Fat: 14 g, Carbohydrates: 1 g, Sugar: 0 g, Cholesterol: 135 mg, Sodium: 40 mg.

BEEF WELLINGTON

🕐 60 Min   🍴 2 Servings

Ingredients

- 1 pound of beef tenderloin, trimmed
- 1 tablespoon olive oil
- 2 tablespoons Dijon mustard
- 8 ounces of mushrooms, finely chopped
- 4 slices prosciutto
- 1 sheet puff pastry, thawed
- 1 egg, beaten
- Salt and pepper, to taste

Cooking Instructions

1. Season beef with salt and pepper, sear in olive oil for 2 minutes on each side.
2. Brush with mustard and cool. Sauté mushrooms until dry and cool. Lay prosciutto on plastic wrap, spread mushrooms, place beef on top, and roll tightly. Chill for 15 minutes.
3. Roll out puff pastry, place beef in center, fold pastry over, and seal edges with beaten egg.
4. Brush with egg wash and make slits on top.
5. Preheat your air fryer to 400°F (200°C) and cook beef Wellington for 20-25 minutes until golden brown. Rest for 10 minutes before slicing.
6. Serve and enjoy your Beef Wellington!

Useful Tips

Ensure beef is well-chilled before wrapping in pastry. It can last up to 2 weeks in the fridge.

Nutrition Facts for 1 Serving

Calories: 600 Kcal, Protein: 30 g, Fat: 40 g, Carbohydrates: 30 g, Sugar: 3 g, Cholesterol: 150mg, Sodium: 800 mg.

JUICY PORK CHOPS

🕐 17 Min   🍽 4 Chops

Ingredients

- 4 pork chops
- 2 tablespoons of finely grated Parmesan cheese
- 1/2 tablespoon of sunflower or vegetable oil
- 1/2 teaspoon of dried oregano
- 1/2 teaspoon of paprika
- 1/2 teaspoon of mustard powder
- 1/2 teaspoon of onion powder
- Cooked greens and peas, to serve (optional)

Cooking Instructions

1. Preheat the air fryer to 375°F (190°C). Drizzle the pork chops with oil and rub to coat evenly.
2. Mix the oregano, paprika, mustard powder, onion powder, Parmesan, salt, and black pepper. Sprinkle this mixture over the pork chops to coat them thoroughly.
3. Place the chops in the air fryer basket and cook for 5 minutes. Flip them over and cook for an additional 5-8 minutes until fully cooked. Cooking time may vary based on the thickness and whether the chops are bone-in. Ensure the internal temperature reaches 165°F (75°C).
4. Serve with wilted greens and peas, if desired. And enjoy your Juicy Pork Chops!

Useful Tips

Let the pork come to room temperature by taking it out of the fridge 30 minutes before cooking. It helps ensure even cooking.
It will keep well for up to 3-4 days.

Nutrition Facts for 1 Chop

Calories: 215 Kcal, Protein: 37 g, Fat: 8 g, Carbohydrates: 1 g, Sugar: 0 g, Cholesterol: 90 mg, Sodium: 180 mg

TENDER BABY BACK RIBS

🕐 40 Min   🍽 4 Servings

Ingredients

- 3 pounds of baby back pork ribs
- 1/3 cup of barbeque sauce
- 1 tablespoon of brown sugar
- 1 tablespoon of white sugar
- 1 teaspoon of sweet paprika
- 1 teaspoon of smoked paprika
- 1 teaspoon of granulated garlic
- 1/2 teaspoon of ground black pepper
- 1/2 teaspoon of ground cumin
- 1/2 teaspoon of granulated onion
- 1/4 teaspoon of Greek seasoning (optional)

Cooking Instructions

1. Preheat the air fryer to 350°F (175°C).
2. Remove the membrane from the ribs and cut them into four pieces. Mix brown sugar, white sugar, sweet paprika, smoked paprika, granulated garlic, pepper, cumin, onion, and Greek seasoning in a bowl. Rub the spice mixture onto the ribs.
3. Place the ribs in the air fryer basket and cook for 30 minutes, flipping halfway. Brush with barbecue sauce and air fry for 5 minutes.
4. Serve and enjoy your Tender Baby Back Ribs!

Useful Tips

Let the pork come to room temperature by taking it out of the fridge 30 minutes before cooking. This helps ensure even cooking.
It will keep well for up to 3-4 days.

Nutrition Facts for 1 Serving

Calories: 615 Kcal, Protein: 37 g, Fat: 44 g, Carbohydrates: 16g, Cholesterol: 176mg, Sugar: 12g, Sodium: 415 mg.

BACON WRAPPED SAUSAGES

🕐 35 Min + 4 Hours   🍴 40 Pieces

Ingredients

- 2 packages (8 ounces each) of thawed fully cooked breakfast sausage links
- 3/4 pound of bacon strips
- 1/2 cup + 2 tablespoons of packed brown sugar

Cooking Instructions

1. Cut sausages widthwise in half, and cut bacon strips in half too. Wrap each sausage half with a piece of bacon.
2. Transfer 1/2 cup of brown sugar to a shallow bowl. Roll each bacon-sausage in sugar and secure it with a toothpick. Put all of them in a large bowl and refrigerate for at least 4 hours or overnight.
3. Preheat your air fryer to 325°F.
4. Put the first batch of sausages inside the preheated basket, sprinkle over them 1 tablespoon of brown sugar, and air fry them at 325°F for 15-20 minutes, turning halfway through cooking, until crispy bacon.
5. Serve warm and enjoy your Bacon Wrapped Sausages!

Useful Tips

You can keep the leftovers in an airtight food container in a fridge for up to 3-4 days. Just reheat them at 325°F for 2-3 minutes.

Nutrition Facts for 1 Piece

Calories: 74 Kcal, Protein: 2 g, Fat: 6 g, Carbohydrates: 4 g, Sugar: 4 g, Cholesterol: 9 mg, Sodium: 154 mg.

ROAST PORK

🕐 1 Hour 20 Min   🍴 4-6 Servings

Ingredients

- 3 pounds of roast pork leg
- 1-2 tablespoons of coarse salt
- 1 tablespoon of olive oil

Cooking Instructions

1. Remove the roast from the packaging. Use paper towels to pat the roast dry, removing excess moisture. Take a small sharp knife and score the rind of the roast at 1 cm intervals. Be cautious not to cut into the meat while scoring.
2. Leave the meat uncovered in the refrigerator for at least 1 hour or overnight. It allows the surface of the meat to dry out, especially the rind, which is crucial for achieving crispy crackling.
3. Rub the meat with olive oil and salt, being sure to get into the scores.
4. Place it inside your air fryer basket and roast at 400°F for 20 minutes, then at 350°F until fully cooked (about 25 minutes for every 1 pound).
5. Let it cool for 10 minutes before slicing.
6. Serve and enjoy your Roast Pork!

Useful Tips

Keep the leftovers in an airtight food container in a fridge for up to 5 days.

Nutrition Facts for 1 Serving

Calories: 750 Kcal, Protein: 58 g, Fat: 56 g, Carbohydrates: 0 g, Cholesterol: 225 mg, Sugar: 9 g.

BEEF KABOBS

🕐 40 Min   🍴 8 Kabobs

Ingredients

- 1 pound of beef chuck ribs (cut into 1-inch pieces, or any other tender cut meat (think steak or stew meat)
- 1 bell pepper
- 1/2 onion
- 1/3 cup of low-fat sour cream
- 2 tablespoons of soy sauce
- 8 six-inch skewers

Cooking Instructions

1. In a medium bowl, blend sour cream with soy sauce. Add the beef chunks and let them marinate* for at least 30 minutes, or preferably overnight.
2. Chop bell peppers and onions into 1-inch pieces. Soak wooden skewers in water for around 10 minutes.
3. Skewer the onions, beef, sprinkle, and bell peppers with freshly ground black pepper.
4. Place the skewers in a preheated air fryer at 400°F (205°C) and cook for 10 minutes, turning them halfway through the cooking time.
5. Serve and enjoy your Beef Kabobs!

Useful Tips

* Marinating for at least 30 minutes makes this dish so full of flavor.

Store leftovers in an airtight container in the refrigerator for up to 4 days.

Nutrition Facts for 1 Serving

Calories: 250 Kcal, Protein: 23 g, Fat: 15 g, Carbohydrates: 4 g, Sugar: 2 g, Cholesterol: 84 mg, Sodium: 609 mg.

CHEESEBURGERS

🕐 30 Min   🍴 4 Burgers

Ingredients

- 1 pound of ground beef
- 1 tablespoon of low-sodium soy sauce
- 2 minced garlic cloves
- 4 slices of American cheese
- 4 hamburger buns
- Mayonnaise
- Lettuce
- Sliced tomatoes
- Thinly sliced red onion
- Kosher salt
- Freshly ground black pepper

Cooking Instructions

1. In a large bowl, mix the minced garlic, ground beef, and soy sauce. Form the mixture into 4 patties, each flattened into a 4-inch circle. Season both sides with salt and pepper.
2. Place 2 patties in the air fryer and cook at 375°F (190°C) for 4 minutes on each side for medium doneness. Remove and immediately place a slice of cheese on top. Repeat with the remaining 2 patties.
3. Spread mayonnaise on the toasted* hamburger buns, then assemble with lettuce, patties, tomatoes, and thinly sliced red onion.
4. Serve and enjoy your Cheeseburgers!

Useful Tips

Store in the refrigerator for 4-5 days.

Nutrition Facts for 1 Burger

Calories: 645 Kcal, Protein: 32 g, Fat: 43 g, Carbohydrates: 32 g, Sugar: 5 g, Cholesterol: 118 mg, Sodium: 1239 mg.

EASY HOT DOG

🕐 20 Min   🍽 8 Hot Dogs

Ingredients

- 8 hot dogs
- 8 hot dog buns
- Mustard, relish, and ketchup, for serving

Cooking Instructions

1. Preheat the air fryer to 400°F (205°C).
2. Air fry the hot dogs in 2 batches (4 at a time), turning halfway through, for 5 to 6 minutes until they are crisp and heated through. Use a paper towel to wipe grease from the base of the air fryer basket.
3. Place the hot dogs in the buns. Air fry in two batches until the buns are toasted, about 1 to 2 minutes.
4. Serve hot with mustard, relish, ketchup, or your favorite toppings! enjoy your Hot Dogs!

Useful Tips

This air fryer method is effective for all types of hot dogs, including standard ballpark franks, turkey dogs, and plant-based varieties.

Leftover portions can be refrigerated and kept for 4 days.

Nutrition Facts for 1 Hot Dog

Calories: 262 Kcal, Protein: 10 g, Fat: 14 g, Carbohydrates: 22 g, Sugar: 3 g, Cholesterol: 23 mg, Sodium: 627 mg.

BACON JALAPEÑO POPPERS

🕐 45 Min   🍽 24 Servings

Ingredients

- 12 jalapeños
- 12 slices of bacon, halved
- 1 1/2 cups of shredded pepper jack cheese*
- 1 (8-ounce) block of cream cheese, softened
- 1 minced garlic clove
- Kosher salt
- Freshly cracked black pepper

Cooking Instructions

1. In a large bowl, mix together the pepper jack cheese, cream cheese, and minced garlic. Season with salt and pepper to taste.
2. Halve the jalapeños lengthwise and use a spoon to remove the seeds and veins. Fill each half with the cheese mixture and wrap a halved slice of bacon around each one.
3. Place the jalapeños in a single layer in the air fryer basket, working in batches if necessary. Cook at 400°F (205°C) for 10 to 12 minutes, until the cheese is bubbly and the bacon is fully cooked.
4. Serve and enjoy your Bacon Jalapeño Poppers!

Useful Tips

* Pepper jack is a great addition to the cream cheese mixture for extra heat, but if that's not preferred, another cheese can be used.

Store any leftovers in an airtight container in the fridge for up to 3 days.

Nutrition Facts for 1 Serving

Calories: 119 Kcal, Protein: 4 g, Fat: 11 g, Carbohydrates: 1 g, Sugar: 1 g, Cholesterol: 25 mg, Sodium: 181 mg.

PORK TENDERLOIN

🕐 30 Min   🍴 4 Servings

Ingredients

- 1 1/2 pounds of pork tenderloin
- 2 teaspoons of kosher salt
- 2 teaspoons of light brown sugar
- 1 teaspoon of ground black pepper
- 1 teaspoon of dried thyme
- 1 teaspoon of paprika
- 1/2 teaspoon of garlic powder
- 1 tablespoon of olive oil

Cooking Instructions

1. Remove pork tenderloin from the fridge, pat dry, and cut in half. Mix salt, brown sugar, pepper, thyme, paprika, and garlic powder in a bowl. Rub olive oil on the tenderloin and coat with the spice mixture.
2. Place the tenderloin pieces in the air fryer basket with space between them. Cook at 400°F (205°C) for 10 minutes, flip, then cook at 355°F (180°C) for 10-15 minutes until internal temperature reaches 145°F (65°C).
3. Let rest for 5 minutes before slicing. Serve and enjoy your Pork Tenderloin!

Useful Tips

Salt, sugar, and pepper are essential for the spice rub, but you can vary the other ingredients depending on what you have in your spice cabinet.

Store leftovers in the refrigerator for up to 4-5 days.

Nutrition Facts for 1 Serving

Calories: 245 Kcal, Protein: 35 g, Fat: 9 g, Carbohydrates: 2 g, Sugar: 2 g, Cholesterol: 111 mg, Sodium: 411 mg.

HONEY GLAZED HAM

🕐 55 Min   🍴 4 Servings

Ingredients

- 1 small smoked ham (about 3 pounds)
- 2 tablespoons of honey
- 1 tablespoon of brown sugar
- 1 tablespoon of orange juice or pineapple juice
- 2 teaspoons of Dijon mustard (optional)

Cooking Instructions

1. Preheat the air fryer to 320°F (160°C).
2. Wrap the ham in foil, ensuring it doesn't touch the top of the air fryer. If necessary, cut the ham in half horizontally.
3. Place the wrapped ham* in the air fryer with the foil seam facing up. Cook for 25 minutes.
4. In a small bowl, mix the glaze ingredients and brush over the ham.
5. Reseal the foil and cook for an additional 10-15 minutes until the ham reaches 135°F (60°C).
6. Uncover the foil* and cook for another 5-10 minutes to brown the glaze.
7. Serve and enjoy your Honey Glazed Ham!

Useful Tips

* Wrap ham in foil. Make sure the foil does not touch the air fryer heating element. If necessary, trim the ham from the bottom to fit.

Leftovers should be tightly wrapped in plastic and stored in ziplock bags. They can be kept in the refrigerator for 3-5 days or in the freezer for up to two months.

Nutrition Facts for 1 Serving

Calories: 47 Kcal, Protein: 0 g, Fat: 0 g, Carbohydrates: 12 g, Sugar: 12 g, Cholesterol: 0 mg, Sodium: 32 mg.

SEAFOOD

HONEY GLAZED SALMON

🕐 50 Min   🍴 4 Servings

Ingredients

- 16 ounces of salmon filets
- 3 tablespoons of honey
- 2 tablespoons of soy sauce
- 2 tablespoons of olive oil
- 2 tablespoons of minced garlic
- 1 teaspoon of ginger
- 1/2 teaspoon of black pepper
- 1/2 teaspoon of red pepper flakes
- Green onion, for garnish
- Lemon or lime, for garnish

Cooking Instructions

1. In a small bowl, whisk together olive oil, minced garlic, honey, soy sauce, ground black pepper, grated ginger, and red pepper flakes (if using).
2. Place salmon fillets in a dish or plastic bag and pour half the glaze over them, reserving the rest. Coat evenly, cover, and refrigerate for at least 30 minutes.
3. Preheat the air fryer to 400°F (205°C). Remove the salmon from the marinade, shake off excess, and place it in the air fryer basket. Air fry for 8-10 minutes, basting with the reserved glaze halfway through. Enjoy Honey Glazed Salmon!

Useful Tips

Store in the refrigerator for up to 4-5 days.

Nutrition Facts for 1 Serving

Calories: 284 Kcal, Protein: 24 g, Fat: 24 g, Carbohydrates: 15 g, Sugar: 13 g, Cholesterol: 49 mg, Sodium: 330 mg.

CILANTRO LIME SHRIMP

🕐 20 Min   🍴 4 Servings

Ingredients

- 1 pound of peeled and deveined shrimp
- 2 tablespoons of olive oil
- 1/4 cup of chopped cilantro
- Zest from one lime
- Juice from one lime
- 3 minced garlic cloves
- 1/2 teaspoon of kosher salt
- 1/4 teaspoon of black pepper

Cooking Instructions

1. Mix shrimp with lime zest, olive oil, garlic, lime juice, salt, cilantro, and pepper. Marinate for 10 minutes.
2. Preheat air fryer to 400°F (205°C). Cook shrimp in a single layer for 5-7 minutes until pink and firm.
3. Garnish with cilantro and lime wedges.
4. Serve and enjoy Cilantro Lime Shrimp!

Useful Tips

Lay shrimp in a single layer in the air fryer basket to avoid overcrowding and ensure even cooking with a slight crispiness.

Enjoy fresh or refrigerate in an airtight container for up to 2 days.

Nutrition Facts for 1 Serving

Calories: 146 Kcal, Protein: 16 g, Fat: 8 g, Carbohydrates: 2 g, Sugar: 0 g, Cholesterol: 142 mg, Sodium: 697 mg.

COCONUT SHRIMP

🕐 20 Min 　　 🍴 4 Servings

Ingredients

- 1 pound of raw shrimp
- 1 cup of shredded coconut*
- 2 eggs
- 1/2 cup of all-purpose flour
- 1 teaspoon of garlic powder
- 1/2 teaspoon of paprika
- 1/2 teaspoon of salt
- 1/2 teaspoon of black pepper

Cooking Instructions

1. Preheat air fryer to 400°F (205°C). Set up three bowls: one with shredded coconut, garlic powder, paprika, salt, and black pepper; one with flour; and one with beaten eggs.
2. Coat shrimp in flour, eggs, and coconut mixture. Place on a tray. Spray the air fryer basket with cooking spray and arrange the shrimp in a single layer.
3. Air fry for 8-10 minutes, flipping halfway, until golden and crispy. Serve hot with herbs or toasted coconut and dipping sauce.
4. Enjoy your Coconut Shrimp!

Useful Tips

* You can choose either sweetened or unsweetened coconut flakes for the breading.

Shrimp is best enjoyed fresh but can be refrigerated in an airtight container for up to 2 days.

Nutrition Facts for 1 Serving

Calories: 162 Kcal, Protein: 5 g, Fat: 9 g, Carbohydrates: 16 g, Sugar: 1 g, Cholesterol: 235 mg, Sodium: 736 mg.

SCALLOPS

🕐 8 Min 　　 🍴 1 Serving

Ingredients

- 1/2 pound of scallops
- 1 teaspoon of salt-free lemon pepper seasoning
- 1/2 teaspoon of paprika
- Salt and pepper to taste
- 1 tablespoon of softened butter

Cooking Instructions

1. Start by preheating your air fryer to 400°F (205°C).
2. Once preheated, spray the air fryer basket with cooking spray.
3. Season both sides of the scallops with salt-free lemon pepper seasoning, paprika, salt, and pepper.
4. Place the scallops in the air fryer and cook for 6 minutes, flipping them after 3 minutes.
5. Toss the scallops with some softened butter. Serve and enjoy your Scallops!

Useful Tips

Be sure to pat dry the scallops with a paper towel before cooking.

Keep the leftovers in an airtight container and refrigerate them for up to 2 days.

Nutrition Facts for 1 Serving

Calories: 257 Kcal, Protein: 27 g, Fat: 12 g, Carbohydrates: 7 g, Sugar: 0 g, Cholesterol: 85 mg, Sodium: 989 mg.

CRAB CAKES

🕐 30 Min   🍴 4 Servings

Ingredients

- 1 pound of jumbo lump crab meat, picked over
- 1 cup of cracker crumbs (about 20 crackers)
- 1 large egg
- 1/4 cup of mayonnaise
- 2 tablespoons of minced chives
- 2 teaspoons of Dijon mustard
- 2 teaspoons of herb seasoning
- 1 teaspoon of finely grated lemon zest
- 1/2 teaspoon of kosher salt
- Tartar sauce, hot sauce, and lemon wedges, for serving.

Cooking Instructions

1. In a large bowl, whisk together egg, mustard, mayonnaise, lemon zest, chives, herb seasoning, and salt. Gently fold in crab meat and cracker crumbs until well combined.
2. Shape the crab mixture into 8 patties. Refrigerate the patties for up to 4 hours if needed.
3. Spray the air-fryer basket and the tops of the crab cakes with cooking spray. Place the crab cakes in a single layer in the basket. Cook at 375°F (190°C), flipping halfway through, until they are deep golden brown and crisp, about 12 to 14 minutes.
4. Serve the warm crab cakes with hot sauce, lemon wedges, and tartar sauce. Enjoy your Crab Cakes!

Useful Tips

Store your crab cakes in the fridge for 2-3 days.

Nutrition Facts for 1 Serving

Calories: 338 Kcal, Protein: 23 g, Fat: 28 g, Carbohydrates: 9 g, Sugar: 2 g, Cholesterol: 168 mg, Sodium: 1139 mg.

PESTO SALMON

🕐 15 Min   🍴 4 Filets

Ingredients

- 4 (4-6 ounces) salmon filets
- 1 tablespoon of avocado oil
- Salt and pepper to season
- 1/3 cup of shredded parmesan cheese
- 1 garlic clove
- 1/4 teaspoon of pepper
- 1/2 cup of olive oil
- 2 cups of fresh-packed basil
- 1/4 cup of pecans
- 1 teaspoon of lemon zest
- 1/2 teaspoon of salt

Cooking Instructions

1. Blend pecans, basil, garlic, lemon zest, salt, and pepper, then slowly add olive oil until smooth. Stir in parmesan cheese.
2. Preheat your air fryer to 400°F (205°C). Pat the salmon dry, brush it with avocado oil, and season. Air fry it skin-side down for 9-10 minutes.
3. Top with pesto. Serve and enjoy your Pesto Salmon!

Useful Tips

Keep an eye on your salmon while cooking, as cook times can vary based on thickness, and aim for an internal temperature of 145°F (65°C) for tender and flaky results.

Store your salmon in an airtight container in the fridge for 2-3 days.

Nutrition Facts for 1 Filet

Calories: 521 Kcal, Protein: 35 g, Fat: 41 g, Carbohydrates: 1 g, Sugar: 0 g, Cholesterol: 5 mg.

FRIED CALAMARI

🕐 15 Min   🍴 4 Servings

Ingredients

- 1 pound of cleaned and skins removed calamari
- 6 cups of avocado oil
- 1 1/2 cups of cold water
- 1 cup of cassava flour
- 1/2 cup of tapioca flour
- 2 large egg whites
- 1 tablespoon of baking soda
- Kosher salt
- 1/2 teaspoon of freshly ground black pepper
- 1 lemon
- 1/2 cup of marinara sauce, optionally

Cooking Instructions

1. Preheat air fryer to 400°F (205°C).
2. Spray the basket with avocado oil, arrange the calamari in a single layer, and spray them thoroughly.
3. Cook for 6-8 minutes, shaking halfway, until golden and crunchy.
4. Season with salt and serve with lemon and marinara sauce. Enjoy your Fried Calamari!

Useful Tips

To get perfect fried calamari from the air fryer, spray a generous coat of avocado oil on the squid before cooking, shake the basket midway, and start checking at the 6-minute mark to avoid overcooking. Place it in an airtight container and refrigerate it for up to 2 days.

Nutrition Facts for 1 Serving

Calories: 280 Kcal, Protein: 20 g, Fat: 15 g, Carbohydrates: 16 g, Sugar: 1 g, Cholesterol: 237 mg, Sodium: 747 mg.

JUICY FISH

🕐 32 Min   🍴 6 Servings

Ingredients

- 1 pound of fresh or frozen cod* (approximately 2 filets)
- 3 large eggs
- 3/4 cup of plain bread crumbs
- 1/4 cup of all-purpose flour
- 3 tablespoons of olive oil
- 1 tablespoon of herb seasoning
- 1 teaspoon of kosher salt

Cooking Instructions

1. Preheat air fryer to 400°F (205°C). Pat thawed cod dry and cut into strips.
2. Whisk eggs in one bowl, mix bread crumbs, flour, Old Bay, and salt in another. Dredge fish in egg, then coat in breadcrumb mix, repeating twice.
3. Coat the air fryer basket with olive oil, place the fish, and drizzle with more oil. Cook for 8 minutes, flip, then cook for 4 more minutes until golden.
4. Serve with tartar sauce and lemon. Enjoy your Juicy Fish!

Useful Tips

* You can substitute any white fish for the cod.
Store any leftover air fryer fish in an airtight container in the fridge for up to 3 to 4 days.

Nutrition Facts for 1 Serving

Calories: 230 Kcal, Protein: 19 g, Fat: 10 g, Carbohydrates: 14 g, Sugar: 1 g, Cholesterol: 140 mg, Sodium: 659 mg.

SESAME-CRUSTED TUNA

🕐 10 Min   🍽 1 Steak

Ingredients

- 1 tuna steak (7 ounces)
- 1 teaspoon of sesame oil
- 2 tablespoons of black sesame seeds
- 2 tablespoons of white sesame seeds
- 1/2 teaspoon of pepper
- 1/2 teaspoon of salt
  For the Wasabi Mayonnaise:
- 1/3 cup of mayonnaise
- 1 teaspoon of soy sauce (or coconut aminos or tamari)
- 2-3 teaspoons of wasabi

Cooking Instructions

1. Preheat your air fryer to 400°F (205°C) for 5 minutes.
2. Mix sesame seeds on a plate. Pat tuna dry, rub with sesame oil, and season with salt and pepper. Coat with sesame seeds, pressing to adhere.
3. Place tuna in the air fryer basket, covered with cooking spray. Cook for 2 minutes, flip, and cook 1 more minute for rare.
4. Mix mayonnaise, wasabi, and soy sauce. Serve and enjoy your Sesame-crusted Tuna Steak!

Useful Tips

* Ensure the sesame seeds are evenly pressed onto the tuna steak to create a uniform crust that enhances the texture and flavor.
Store leftovers in the refrigerator for up to 3 days.

Nutrition Facts for 1 Steak

Calories: 984 Kcal, Protein: 52 g, Fat: 78 g, Carbohydrates: 10g, Cholesterol: 100 mg, Sugar: 0g, Sodium: 1305 mg.

FISH AND CHIPS

🕐 40 Min   🍽 4 Servings

Ingredients

Fish:
- 4 white fish fillets (cod, haddock, or pollock)
- 1/2 cup flour
- 1 egg
- 1 cup panko breadcrumbs
  Chips:
- 2 large potatoes*
- 1 tablespoon of olive oil
- Salt and pepper to taste

Cooking Instructions

1. Peel and cut potatoes into 1/2-inch sticks. Toss with olive oil, salt, and pepper. Air fry at 375°F (190°C) for 20-25 minutes.
2. Coat fish in flour, dip in beaten egg, and coat with panko. Spray with cooking spray. Air fry at 375°F (190°C) for 10-12 minutes.
3. Serve warm with your favorite dipping sauce. Enjoy your Fish and Chips!

Useful Tips

* The best potatoes for fries are those with a high starch content. Idaho or Russet potatoes are top choices, though all-purpose Yukon Gold potatoes are also good for frying.
Keep the fish fillets in an airtight container in the refrigerator for 3-4 days.

Nutrition Facts for 1 Serving

Calories: 312 Kcal, Protein: 23 g, Fat: 9 g, Carbohydrates: 35 g, Sugar: 3 g, Cholesterol: 85 mg, Sodium: 503 mg.

SHRIMP TEMPURA

🕐 12 Min   🍽 6 Servings

Ingredients

- 2 pounds of raw peeled shrimp (medium or large size)
- 2 1/2 cups of Panko bread crumbs
- 1 cup of all-purpose flour
- 2 tablespoons of vegetable oil
- 2 eggs
- 2 teaspoons of water

Cooking Instructions

1. Preheat the air fryer to 355°F (180°C).
2. Whisk together 2 large eggs and 2 teaspoons of water to make an egg wash.
3. Coat the shrimp in flour, shaking off any excess.
4. Dip the floured shrimp into the egg wash, then coat with panko breadcrumbs.
5. Cook the shrimp in the air fryer for 7 to 9 minutes, or until they are fully cooked.
6. Serve and enjoy your Shrimp Tempura!

Useful Tips

If you can't lay the shrimp out in a single layer, it's best to cook them in small batches.

Store leftovers in an airtight container in the refrigerator for up to 4 days.

Nutrition Facts for 1 Serving

Calories: 387 Kcal, Protein: 38 g, Fat: 10 g, Carbohydrates: 34g, Sugar: 2g, Cholesterol: 436 mg, Sodium: 1379 mg.

TUNA PATTIES

🕐 50 Min   🍽 4 Servings

Ingredients

- 2 cans of drained tuna
- 1 egg
- 1/4 cup breadcrumbs
- 2 tablespoons of mayonnaise
- 1 tablespoon of Dijon mustard
- Salt and pepper to taste

Cooking Instructions

1. Preheat the air fryer to 400°F (205°C).
2. Mix together 2 cans of drained tuna, 1 egg, 1/4 cup of breadcrumbs, 2 tablespoons of mayonnaise, 1 tablespoons of Dijon mustard, salt, and pepper.
3. Shape the mixture into 4-6 patties.
4. Spray the air fryer basket with cooking spray. Place patties in a single layer and spray the tops lightly.
5. Cook the patties for 8-10 minutes, flipping halfway through, until golden brown.
6. Serve hot and enjoy your Tuna Patties!

Useful Tips

Use a combination of breadcrumbs and eggs to bind the patties together. This helps in maintaining their shape during cooking.

Store leftovers in an airtight container in the refrigerator for up to 4 days.

Nutrition Facts for 1 Serving

Calories: 335 Kcal, Protein: 22 g, Fat: 15 g, Carbohydrates: 14 g, Sugar: 2 g, Cholesterol: 95 mg, Sodium: 470 mg.

VEGETABLE MAINS & SIDES

CRISPY POTATO WEDGES

🕐 30 Min   🍴 4 Servings

Ingredients

- 1 1/2 pounds of small russet potatoes (roughly 3-4 potatoes)
- 1 tablespoon of olive oil
- 1/2 teaspoon of paprika
- 1/2 teaspoon of onion powder
- 1/2 teaspoon of garlic powder
- 1/2 teaspoon of salt

Cooking Instructions

1. Select small to medium russet potatoes, avoiding large or long ones. Cut each potato into 8 wedges.
2. Soak the wedges in cold water for 15-30 minutes to remove starch and add moisture.
3. Shake off excess water and blot dry with a towel.
4. Toss the wedges in oil, paprika, onion powder, garlic powder, and salt until evenly coated.
5. Preheat the air fryer to 400°F (205°C).
6. Arrange the wedges cut side down in the air fryer and cook for 7 minutes. Flip and cook for another 3-5 minutes, until edges are crispy and insides are soft.
7. Serve and enjoy your Crispy Potato Wedges!

Useful Tips

Potato wedges can be stored in an airtight container in the fridge for up to 48 hours.

Nutrition Facts for 8 Wedges

Calories: 168 Kcal, Protein: 4 g, Fat: 4 g, Carbohydrates: 31 g, Sugar: 1 g, Cholesterol: 65 mg, Sodium: 300 mg.

CAULIFLOWER TACOS

🕐 55 Min   🍴 4 Servings

Ingredients

- 1 head cauliflower, cut into florets
- 1 cup of almond milk
- 1 cup of panko breadcrumbs
- 1/2 cup of flour
- 1 tablespoon of taco seasoning
- jalapeno
- Salt and pepper, to taste
- 1 avocado
- Cilantro
- 8 small tortillas

Cooking Instructions

1. Mix flour, taco seasoning, salt, and pepper in a bowl. Add almond milk and stir until smooth.
2. Dip cauliflower florets in the milk mixture, shake off excess, then coat in panko.
3. Air fry cauliflower in batches at 400°F (205°C) for 15 minutes, flipping halfway and spraying with cooking oil.
4. Mix vegan mayo, sriracha, and maple syrup in a small bowl.
5. Assemble tacos with slaw*, cooked cauliflower, avocado, cilantro, and jalapeno optionally.
6. Enjoy your Cauliflower Tacos!

Useful Tips

* Slaw is a salad made from shredded cabbage mixed with dressing.
It can be stored for up to 2 days.

Nutrition Facts for 1 Serving

Calories: 361 Kcal, Protein: 11 g, Fat: 5 g, Carbohydrates: 35g, Sugar: 6g, Cholesterol: 289 mg.

TOFU SALAD

⏱ 45 Min   🍴 4 Servings

Ingredients

- 14 ounces of extra firm tofu*
- 1 tablespoon of fresh ginger
- 3 minced garlic cloves
- 3 tablespoons of hoisin sauce
- 2 tablespoons of soy sauce
- 2 tablespoons of sugar, or sugar substitute
- 1 tablespoon of vegetable oil
- 1/2 teaspoon of red pepper flakes

Cooking Instructions

1. Marinate the extra firm tofu in the specified ingredients for up to 30 minutes.
2. Place the tofu in a well-oiled 6-inch springform pan.
3. Preheat the air fryer to 400°F (205°C).
4. Cook for 10 minutes, shaking the basket halfway through.
5. Serve and enjoy your Tofu!

Useful Tips

* Choose extra firm tofu, as other types may release excess liquid, making it difficult to achieve crispy edges.

Store leftovers in an airtight container in the refrigerator for up to 3-4 days.

Nutrition Facts for 1 Serving

Calories: 204 Kcal, Protein: 12 g, Fat: 10 g, Carbohydrates: 18g, Sugar: 2g, Cholesterol: 203 mg, Sodium: 680 mg.

EGGPLANT FRIES

⏱ 25 Min   🍴 6 Servings

Ingredients

- 1 medium eggplant (about 1-1/4 pounds)
- 1 cup of meatless pasta sauce, warmed
- 1/2 cup of grated Parmesan cheese
- 1/2 cup of toasted wheat germ
- 2 large eggs
- 1 teaspoon of Italian seasoning
- 3/4 teaspoon of garlic salt
- Cooking spray

Cooking Instructions

1. Preheat air fryer to 375°F (190°C). Whisk eggs in a shallow bowl. In another bowl, mix cheese, wheat germ, Italian seasonings, and garlic salt.
2. Trim eggplant ends and cut into 1/2-inch-thick slices, then into 1/2-inch strips. Dip strips in eggs, then coat in cheese mixture. Place in a single layer on a greased tray in the air fryer basket.
3. Spray tops with cooking spray. Cook for 4-5 minutes until golden brown, flip, spray again, and cook for another 4-5 minutes until golden brown.
4. Serve immediately with pasta sauce. Enjoy your Eggplant Fries!

Useful Tips

Eggplant skin can become more bitter with age, so if you're using an older eggplant, consider peeling it before frying.

Store leftovers in an airtight container in the refrigerator for up to 4 days.

Nutrition Facts for 1 Serving

Calories: 135 Kcal, Protein: 9 g, Fat: 5 g, Carbohydrates: 15 g, Sugar: 6 g, Sodium: 577 mg.

ZESTY LEMON ASPARAGUS

🕐 12 Min   🍴 4 Servings

Ingredients

- 1 bunch of asparagus, ends trimmed
- 1/4 cup of grated Parmesan cheese
- 1 tablespoon of olive oil
- 1 tablespoon of lemon juice
- 1 teaspoon of lemon zest
- Salt and pepper, to taste

Cooking Instructions

1. Preheat the air fryer to 400°F (205°C).
2. Toss the asparagus with olive oil, lemon juice, lemon zest, Parmesan cheese, and salt and pepper to taste.
3. Place the asparagus onto the preheated crisper plate and cook for 7 minutes.
4. Remove the asparagus when golden brown and crisp-tender.
5. Serve and enjoy your Zesty Lemon Asparagus!

Useful Tips

Arrange the asparagus in a single layer in the air fryer basket. Avoid overcrowding to ensure the spears cook evenly and become crisp.

Store the container in the refrigerator. The asparagus will stay fresh for up to 3-4 days.

Nutrition Facts for 1 Serving

Calories: 74 Kcal, Protein: 4 g, Fat: 5 g, Carbohydrates: 4 g, Sugar: 1 g, Cholesterol: 7 mg, Sodium: 204 mg.

HONEY CARROTS

🕐 18 Min   🍴 4 Servings

Ingredients

- 1 pound of baby carrots
- 2 tablespoons of honey
- 4 tablespoons of melted butter
- 2 finely minced garlic cloves
- 1/4 teaspoon of red pepper flakes (optional)
- Salt and pepper, to taste
- Cooking spray

Cooking Instructions

1. Preheat your air fryer to 360°F (185°C) for 5 minutes. Coat carrots with melted butter, then season with salt and pepper. Spray the air fryer basket with cooking spray and arrange the carrots in a single layer. Cook for 8 minutes.
2. While cooking, mix the remaining melted butter, garlic, honey, and red pepper flakes to make honey butter garlic sauce.
3. Toss cooked carrots with sauce and cook for 5-6 more minutes.
4. Adjust seasoning and garnish with fresh parsley if desired.
5. Serve and enjoy your Honey Carrots!

Useful Tips

For extra caramelization, cook the carrots a few minutes longer.

Keep in the refrigerator for up to 4-5 days.

Nutrition Facts for 1 Serving

Calories: 175 Kcal, Protein: 1 g, Fat: 12 g, Carbohydrates: 19 g, Sugar: 14 g, Cholesterol: 30mg, Sodium: 181 mg.

MEXICAN CORN

⏱ 20 Min   🍴 4 Corns

Ingredients

- 4 ears of corn on the cob
- 3/4 cup of mayo
- juice of 1/2 lime
- 1 chipotle pepper finely minced in adobo sauce
- cotija cheese
- tajin seasoning
- cilantro, for garnishing (optional)

Cooking Instructions

1. Preheat your air fryer to 400°F (205°C) and coat the air fryer basket with cooking spray. While the air fryer heats up, prepare the chipotle mayo sauce. Combine mayo, lime juice, and minced chipotle pepper in a small bowl.
2. Place the corn in the air fryer basket and cook for 10 minutes, flipping halfway through.
3. Once done, remove the corn from the air fryer and brush it with the chipotle mayo mixture. Sprinkle cotija cheese, cilantro, and tajin on top.
4. Serve your Mexican Corn! And enjoy while still warm!

Useful Tips

Before adding the chipotle mayo sauce, lightly coat the corn with butter to enhance its richness.
Store the corn in the refrigerator for up to 3-4 days.

Nutrition Facts for 1 Corn

Calories: 366 Kcal, Protein: 3 g, Fat: 33 g, Carbohydrates: 18 g, Sugar: 6 g, Cholesterol: 18 mg, Sodium: 280 mg.

THREE CHEESE ARANCINI

⏱ 20 Min   🍴 8 Servings

Ingredients

- 2 cups of cooked risotto
- 1/2 cup of mozzarella cheese, cubed
- 1/4 cup of Parmesan cheese, grated
- 1/4 cup of ricotta cheese
- 1 egg, beaten
- 1/2 cup of flour
- 1 cup of breadcrumbs
- Salt and pepper to taste

Cooking Instructions

1. Preheat the air fryer to 400°F (200°C).
2. Mix cooked risotto with grated Parmesan cheese, ricotta cheese, salt, and pepper.
3. Shape the mixture into balls, inserting a cube of mozzarella in the center of each.
4. Dredge each ball in flour, dip in beaten egg, and coat with breadcrumbs.
5. Spray the air fryer basket with cooking spray. Place arancini in a single layer and spray the tops lightly.
6. Cook for 10-12 minutes, shaking halfway through, until golden brown.
7. Serve hot and enjoy your Three Cheese Arancini!

Useful Tips

Allow the arancini to cool completely to room temperature after cooking. Store in the refrigerator for up to 3-4 days.

Nutrition Facts for 1 Serving

Calories: 249 Kcal, Protein: 10 g, Fat: 11 g, Carbohydrates: 26 g, Sugar: 2 g, Cholesterol: 48 mg, Sodium: 352 mg.

WHOLE CAULIFLOWER

🕐 40 Min   🍴 4 Servings

Ingredients

- 1 whole cauliflower
- 2 tablespoons of olive oil
- 1 teaspoon of salt
- 1/2 teaspoon of black pepper
- 1/2 teaspoon of paprika
- 1/2 cup tahini
- 2 tablespoons of lemon juice
- 1 garlic clove, minced
- 1/4 cup of water
- Fresh parsley for garnish

Cooking Instructions

1. Preheat the air fryer to 375°F (190°C).
2. Trim the leaves and stem of the cauliflower, leaving the core intact.
3. Rub the cauliflower with olive oil, salt, black pepper, and paprika.
4. Place the cauliflower in the air fryer basket and cook for 20-25 minutes, until tender and golden brown.
5. In a bowl, whisk together tahini, lemon juice, minced garlic, and water until smooth.
6. Drizzle the tahini sauce over the roasted cauliflower and garnish with fresh parsley.
7. Serve and enjoy your Whole Cauliflower.

Useful Tips

Allow the roasted cauliflower to rest briefly before slicing or serving.
It will keep well for up to 3-4 days.

Nutrition Facts for 1 Serving

Calories: 350 Kcal, Protein: 12 g, Fat: 27 g, Carbohydrates: 22 g, Sugar: 2 g, Cholesterol: 6 mg, Sodium: 180 mg.

CAULIFLOWER BITES

🕐 30 Min   🍴 4 Servings

Ingredients

- 1 cauliflower
- 3/4 cup of plain flour
- 7 fluid ounces of milk
- 1 teaspoon of garlic powder
- 1 teaspoon of onion powder
- 1 teaspoon of paprika
- 1/3 cup of hot sauce
- 1 tablespoon of honey

Cooking Instructions

1. Wash and cut cauliflower into small florets, varying sizes are fine.
2. Mix flour, milk, garlic, onion powder, and paprika in a bowl. Coat cauliflower thoroughly.
3. Place coated cauliflower in the air fryer with 1 tablespoon of oil. Cook at 375°F (190°C) for 15 minutes.
4. Heat hot sauce and honey in a pan until bubbling. Toss cooked cauliflower in buffalo sauce.
5. Serve and enjoy your Cauliflower Bites!

Useful Tips

Arrange the cauliflower bites in a single layer without overcrowding to allow air to circulate evenly for crispier results.
Place the cooled cauliflower bites in an airtight container or a sealed plastic bag. Store them in the refrigerator for up to 3-4 days.

Nutrition Facts for 1 Serving

Calories: 190 Kcal, Protein: 7 g, Fat: 3 g, Carbohydrates: 35 g, Sugar: 3 g, Cholesterol: 56 mg, Sodium: 634 mg.

CRISPY GREEN BEANS

🕐 15 Min   🍽 4 Servings

Ingredients

- 1 pound of green beans, trimmed and washed
- 1 tablespoon of olive oil
- 1/2 teaspoon of garlic powder
- 1/2 teaspoon of salt
- 1/4 teaspoon of black pepper

Cooking Instructions

1. Preheat the air fryer to 375°F (190°C).
2. In a medium bowl, toss green beans with olive oil, garlic powder, salt, and pepper.
3. Arrange green beans in a single layer in the air fryer basket.
4. Cook for 9 minutes, tossing halfway through. For softer beans, cook an additional 2 minutes.
5. Serve and enjoy your Crispy Green Beans!

Useful Tips

Always ensure the green beans are completely dry before air frying. Water can prevent them from achieving maximum crispiness in the air fryer.
Simply store them in an airtight container in the refrigerator for up to 4 days.

Nutrition Facts for 1 Serving

Calories: 67 Kcal, Protein: 2 g, Fat: 4 g, Carbohydrates: 8 g, Sugar: 4 g, Cholesterol: 0 mg, Sodium: 298 mg.

SWEET POTATO FRIES

🕐 30 Min   🍽 4 Servings

Ingredients

- 2 large sweet potatoes, peeled
- 2 tablespoons of avocado oil
- 1/2 teaspoon of garlic powder
- 1/2 teaspoon of smoked paprika
- 1/4 teaspoon of cinnamon
- 1/2 teaspoon of salt (plus additional for seasoning after fries are cooked)

Cooking Instructions

1. Cut peeled sweet potatoes into thick slices* and soak in water for 30-60 minutes. Pat dry.
2. In a bowl, toss fries with avocado oil, smoked paprika, garlic powder, salt, and optional cinnamon.
3. Preheat your air fryer to 400°F (205°C). Spray the basket with cooking spray. Arrange fries in a single layer. Air fry for 10-12 minutes, shaking halfway.
4. Remove and season with salt if desired. Serve and enjoy your Sweet Potato Fries!

Useful Tips

* Slice the sweet potato lengthwise into 1/4 inch to 1/2 inch thick slices.
Allow your fries to cool to room temperature before storing them in an airtight container in the fridge. They will keep well for up to 3 days.

Nutrition Facts for 1 Serving

Calories: 232 Kcal, Protein: 2 g, Fat: 8 g, Carbohydrates: 17 g, Sugar: 5 g, Cholesterol: 34 mg, Sodium: 235 mg.

POLENTA FRIES

🕐 35 Min   🍴 4 Servings

Ingredients

- 1 package (16 ounces) of prepared polenta
- Nonstick olive oil cooking spray
- Salt and ground black pepper, to taste

Cooking Instructions

1. Preheat your air fryer to 355°F (180°C).
2. Slice the polenta into long, thin slices resembling French fries.
3. Spray the bottom of the basket with cooking spray. Place half of the polenta fries in the basket and lightly mist the tops with cooking spray. Season with salt and pepper.
4. Cook in the preheated air fryer for 10 minutes. Flip the fries with a spatula and cook for about 5 minutes more, until crispy. Transfer the fries to a paper towel-lined plate. Repeat with the remaining fries.
5. Serve and enjoy your Polenta Fries!

Useful Tips

You can also cut the polenta into wedge shapes to mimic potato wedges. Because they are thicker, increase the cooking time by 10 minutes.

Store leftovers in an airtight container in the refrigerator for up to 4 days.

Nutrition Facts for 1 Serving

Calories: 80 Kcal, Protein: 2 g, Fat: 1 g, Carbohydrates: 17 g, Sugar: 1 g, Cholesterol: 122 mg, Sodium: 452 mg.

ZUCCHINI CORN DOGS

🕐 30 Min   🍴 4 Corn Dogs

Ingredients

- 2 medium zucchinis
- 1 cup of cornmeal
- 1/2 cup of flour
- 1 tablespoon of sugar
- 1 teaspoon of baking powder
- 1/2 teaspoon of salt
- 1/2 cup of milk
- 1 egg, beaten
- Wooden skewers
- Cooking spray

Cooking Instructions

1. Preheat the air fryer to 375°F (190°C).
2. Insert wooden skewers into each whole zucchini.
3. In a bowl, mix cornmeal, flour, sugar, baking powder, and salt. Add milk and beaten egg, stirring until smooth.
4. Dip each whole zucchini into the batter, coating evenly.
5. Spray the air fryer basket with cooking spray. Place the coated zucchini in the basket.
6. Cook for 12-15 minutes, turning halfway through,
7. Serve hot and enjoy your Zucchini Corn Dogs!

Useful Tips

Store leftovers in an airtight container in the refrigerator for up to 4 days.

Nutrition Facts for 1 Serving

Calories: 382 Kcal, Protein: 14 g, Fat: 9 g, Carbohydrates: 34 g, Sugar: 2 g, Cholesterol: 88 mg, Sodium: 555 mg.

ZUCCHINI CHIPS

🕐 45 Min   🍴 4 Servings

Ingredients

- 4 medium zucchini
- 1 1/2 tablespoons of olive oil
- 1/2 teaspoon of kosher salt
- 1/4 teaspoon of freshly ground black pepper
  For the Sour Cream Dip:
- 1/4 cup of plain Greek yogurt
- 1 small garlic clove
- 2-3 scallions
- 1/4 teaspoon of kosher salt
- 1/4 teaspoon of freshly ground black pepper
- 1/4 cup of sour cream

Cooking Instructions

1. Preheat air fryer to 400°F (205°C).
2. Slice zucchini into 1/4-inch circles. Toss with olive oil, salt, and pepper.
3. Air fry half the zucchini in a single layer for 20 minutes, then transfer to a plate. Repeat with the remaining zucchini.
4. Mix Greek yogurt, sour cream, garlic, scallions, salt, and pepper for the dip.
5. Serve Zucchini Chips with the dip and enjoy!

Useful Tips

Store leftovers in an airtight container in the refrigerator for up to 4 days.

Nutrition Facts for 1 Serving

Calories: 120 Kcal, Protein: 5 g, Fat: 9 g, Carbohydrates: 8 g, Sugar: 5 g, Sodium: 254 mg, Cholesterol: 9 mg.

PIZZA ROLLS

🕐 8 Min   🍴 8 Rolls

Ingredients

- 1 batch of pizza dough
- 1/2 cup of pizza sauce
- 1-2 cups of shredded mozzarella cheese
- 1 tablespoon of olive oil

Cooking Instructions

1. Follow the instructions to prepare the dough.
2. Place the dough on a floured surface and roll it into a rectangular shape about half an inch thick using a rolling pin.
3. Spread pizza sauce on top, leaving space around the edges.
4. Add cheese and your preferred pizza toppings, then roll the dough jelly roll style.
5. Slice the roll into 8 portions using a wet knife.
6. Lightly grease an air fryer basket, brush the outside of the pizza rolls, and place them in the basket.
7. Air fry at 400°F (205°C) for 8-10 minutes, turning them halfway through.
8. Take the pizza rolls out of the air fryer.
9. Serve warm and enjoy your Pizza Rolls!

Useful Tips

Leftover pizza rolls can be stored in the refrigerator for up to 5 days.

Nutrition Facts for 1 Roll

Calories: 160 Kcal, Protein: 9 g, Fat: 6 g, Carbohydrates: 20 g, Sugar: 1 g, Sodium: 180 mg, Cholesterol: 122 mg.

TOASTED RAVIOLI

🕐 30 Min   🍴 6 Servings

Ingredients

- 2 tablespoons of whole milk
- 1 large egg
- 1 to 1 1/4 cups of warmed marinara sauce
- 2/3 cup of dried Italian-style or plain bread crumbs (not panko)
- Freshly ground black pepper
- Kosher salt
- 1 package (10 ounces) of refrigerated or frozen ravioli, thawed if frozen
- 1/3 cup of finely shredded Parmesan
- Vegetable or peanut oil (for deep frying) or cooking spray (for air frying)

Cooking Instructions

1. Whisk egg and milk in one bowl and mix breadcrumbs with salt and pepper in another.
2. Dip ravioli in egg, coat with breadcrumbs, and arrange on a baking sheet.
3. Heat oil to 355°F (180°C) and fry ravioli in batches for 3 minutes. Drain on paper towels.
4. Preheat your air fryer to 355°F (180°C). Spray basket and ravioli, then air fry for 5-7 minutes.
5. Serve with Parmesan and marinara sauce. Enjoy your Toasted Ravioli!

Useful Tips

Store in the refrigerator for up to 2-3 days.

Nutrition Facts for 1 Serving

Calories: 548 Kcal, Protein: 18 g, Fat: 31 g, Carbohydrates: 48 g, Sugar: 3 g, Sodium: 181 mg, Cholesterol: 62 mg.

GARLIC BAGUETTE

🕐 8 Min   🍴 4 Servings

Ingredients

- 1/2 cup of half-fat butter
- Handful of freshly chopped parsley
- Salt and pepper
- 1/2 cup of reduced-fat mozzarella
- 1 garlic baguette
- 6 grated garlic cloves

Cooking Instructions

1. Prepare a garlic butter spread by combining softened butter, minced garlic, chopped parsley, salt, and pepper*.
2. Slice the bread and fill it with the garlic butter. Rub 2 tablespoons of water across the bread with your fingers if the bread is stale.
3. Air fry for 8 minutes at 355°F (180°C).
4. Serve and enjoy your Garlic Baguette!

Useful Tips

* Enhance the flavor by infusing the butter with additional herbs like thyme, rosemary, or basil.
Store the wrapped baguette in the refrigerator. It can be kept fresh for up to 3-4 days.

Nutrition Facts for 1 Serving

Calories: 160 Kcal, Protein: 4 g, Fat: 10 g, Carbohydrates: 15 g, Sugar: 1 g, Sodium: 322 mg, Cholesterol: 26 mg.

SPICY ONION RINGS

🕐 55 Min   🍴 4 Servings

Ingredients

- 2 large, sweet onions, sliced 1/2 inch thick
  For the batter:
- 1 egg
- 2/3 cup of buttermilk
- 1 teaspoon of chili and lime seasoning blend
- 1/4 cup of all-purpose flour
- 1/2 teaspoon of adobo all-purpose seasoning
  For the breading:
- 2 cups of panko bread crumbs
- 1 teaspoon of adobo all-purpose seasoning
- 1/2 teaspoon of chili and lime seasoning blend
- 1 teaspoon of kosher salt, or to taste

Cooking Instructions

1. Whisk buttermilk, egg, flour, and seasonings for the batter. Refrigerate for 30 minutes.
2. Mix panko and seasonings. Dip onion rings in batter, coat with panko, and cover with cooking spray.
3. Preheat your air fryer to 340°F (170°C). Line the basket with parchment or spray it with oil. Place onion rings in the basket with space between them. Cook for 10-12 minutes, flipping halfway.
4. Keep warm in a 250°F (120°C) oven.
5. Serve and enjoy your Spicy Onion Rings!

Useful Tips

Store leftovers in the refrigerator for up to 3-4 days.

Nutrition Facts for 1 Serving

Calories: 230 Kcal, Protein: 10 g, Fat: 4 g, Carbohydrates: 53 g, Sugar: 1 g, Sodium: 1093 mg, Cholesterol: 48 mg.

FRIED PICKLES

🕐 25 Min   🍴 6 Servings

Ingredients

- 1 jar (16 ounces) of dill pickle coins, drained
- 1 egg
- 1 cup of panko breadcrumbs
- Extra-virgin olive oil, for drizzling
- Remoulade sauce, for dipping

Cooking Instructions

1. Preheat the air fryer to 370°F (190°C).
2. Pat the pickles dry with a clean kitchen towel or paper towels and set aside.
3. In a small bowl, whisk the egg.
4. Place the panko in a medium bowl.
5. Dip each pickle in the whisked egg and coat it with panko. Place the coated pickles on a plate.
6. Lightly drizzle the coated pickles with olive oil.
7. Place the pickles in a single layer in the air fryer basket, ensuring there is space around each one. Work in batches if necessary.
8. Cook for 11 to 14 minutes until crisp and golden brown, adjusting the time based on your air fryer.
9. Serve with remoulade for dipping and enjoy your Fried Pickles!

Useful Tips

Arrange the coated pickles in a single layer in the air fryer basket.

Store the pickles in the refrigerator for up to 3-4 days.

Nutrition Facts for 1 Serving

Calories: 94 Kcal, Protein: 2 g, Fat: 5 g, Carbohydrates: 10 g, Sugar: 2 g, Sodium: 479 mg, Cholesterol: 33 mg.

CRISPY CHICKPEAS

🕐 20 Min   🍴 4 Servings

Ingredients

- 1 can (19 ounces) of chickpeas, drained and rinsed
- 1 tablespoon of olive oil
- 1/8 teaspoon of salt
- 1/4 teaspoon of garlic powder
- 1/4 teaspoon of onion powder
- 1/2 teaspoon of paprika
- 1/4 teaspoon of cayenne (optional)

Cooking Instructions

1. Preheat the air fryer to 390°F (200°C).
2. Drain and rinse the chickpeas, no need to dry them.
3. Toss the chickpeas with olive oil and spices.
4. Place all the chickpeas in the air fryer basket.
5. Cook for 12-15 minutes, shaking the basket a few times during cooking.
6. Once cooked to your liking, remove the chickpeas from the air fryer.
7. Taste and add more salt and pepper if needed.
8. Serve and enjoy your Crispy Chickpeas!

Useful Tips

Store the chickpeas in an open bowl or jar. It helps to keep them crisp by allowing air circulation.

Nutrition Facts for 1 Serving

Calories: 251 Kcal, Protein: 11 g, Fat: 6 g, Carbohydrates: 36 g, Sugar: 6 g, Sodium: 9 mg, Cholesterol: 0 mg.

BROCCOLI RANCH TOTS

🕐 30 Min   🍴 4 Servings

Ingredients

- 1 bag (10 ounces) of frozen broccoli, thawed (about 3 cups)
- 1 1/2 cups of shredded cheddar
- 1 cup of panko breadcrumbs
- 2 tablespoons of ranch seasoning*
- 2 large eggs, beaten to blend
- Olive oil cooking spray
- Ketchup, for serving

Cooking Instructions

1. Pat the broccoli with paper towels, and pulse in a food processor until finely chopped. Transfer to a medium bowl and mix in eggs, cheddar, panko, and ranch seasoning.
2. With a tablespoon measuring spoon and damp hands, scoop out level tablespoonfuls of the mixture and shape into tater tots. Place on a plate.
3. Lightly coat the air fryer basket with cooking spray. Arrange the tots in a single layer, about 1/8" apart, and spray with cooking spray. Cook at 400°F (205°C) for 9 to 11 minutes, turning halfway through and spraying with more cooking spray, until crisp.
4. Serve the tots warm on a platter with ketchup on the side. Enjoy your Broccoli Ranch Tots!

Useful Tips

Store the tots in the refrigerator for up to 3-4 days.

Nutrition Facts for 1 Serving

Calories: 340 Kcal, Protein: 16 g, Fat: 22 g, Carbohydrates: 21 g, Sugar: 4 g, Sodium: 755 mg, Cholesterol: 138 mg.

POTSTICKERS

🕐 1 Hour   🍴 20 Potstickers

Ingredients

- 20 potsticker wrappers
- 1 cup of ground pork or chicken
- 1 cup of shredded cabbage
- 2 green onions, finely chopped
- 1 garlic clove, minced
- 1 teaspoon of fresh ginger, minced
- 1 tablespoon of soy sauce
- 1 teaspoon of sesame oil
- 1/2 teaspoon of salt
- 1/4 teaspoon of black pepper

Cooking Instructions

1. Mix ground pork or chicken with cabbage, green onions, garlic, ginger, soy sauce, sesame oil, salt, and pepper.
2. Spoon filling onto potsticker wrappers. Moisten edges, fold and press to seal.
3. Spray your air fryer basket with cooking spray. Arrange potstickers in a single layer.
4. Lightly spray potstickers with cooking spray.
5. Air fry at 375°F (190°C) for 8-10 minutes, shaking basket halfway, until golden brown and cooked through.
6. Serve hot with soy sauce. Enjoy your Potstickers!

Useful Tips

Store the potstickers in the refrigerator for up to 3-4 days.

Nutrition Facts for 5 Potstickers

Calories: 469 Kcal, Protein: 22 g, Fat: 20 g, Carbohydrates: 52 g, Sugar: 2 g, Sodium: 777 mg, Cholesterol: 49 mg.

JALEBI

🕐 30 Min   🍴 4 Servings

Ingredients

- 3 1/2 ounces of soya flour
- 3 1/2 ounces of puffed rice
- 6 teaspoons of erythritol
- 1 pinch of orange food color
- 1 pinch of salt
- 1 teaspoon of ghee
- 4 cups of water

Cooking Instructions

1. Blend puffed rice, soya flour, salt, food color, water, and ghee until smooth. Let sit for 15-20 minutes, adding water if needed.
2. Fill a nozzle bag with the mixture and create rounds on a greased tray. Air fry at 320°F (160°C) for 7 minutes, then at 355°F (180°C) for 3 minutes.
3. Make syrup by cooking water and erythritol until sticky. Dip baked jalebis in syrup for a few seconds.
4. Serve hot and enjoy your Jalebi!

Useful Tips

Use a piping bag with a small round tip to shape the jalebi into spirals. This helps in achieving uniform shapes and sizes, ensuring even cooking.

If you plan to store them for more than a day, refrigerate the jalebi. They can be stored in the refrigerator for up to 3-4 days.

Nutrition Facts for 1 Serving

Calories: 206 Kcal, Protein: 11 g, Fat: 6 g, Carbohydrates: 30 g, Sugar: 2 g, Sodium: 50 mg, Cholesterol: 3 mg.

CRISPY-COATED MUSHROOMS

🕐 20 Min   🍴 4 Servings

Ingredients

- 1 packet (about 2 ounces) of southern fried chicken coating mix
- 7 ounces of button mushrooms
- 1 cup of thick Greek yogurt
- 2 tablespoons of plain flour
- 1 egg
- 1 tablespoon of milk
- 1 Lebanese cucumber, grated
- Juice of 1 lemon
- Oil spray
  For the dipping sauce:
- 1 cup of thick Greek yogurt
- 1 Lebanese cucumber, grated
- Juice of 1 lemon

Cooking Instructions

1. Dredge mushrooms in flour, then coat in beaten egg and milk mixture, followed by the coating mix.
2. Arrange mushrooms in an air fryer basket, spray with oil, and cook at 390°F (200°C) for 10 minutes until golden.
3. Prepare dipping sauce by mixing ingredients and seasoning to taste.
4. Serve with dipping sauce and enjoy your Crispy-coated Mushrooms!

Useful Tips

Store in the refrigerator for up to 3-4 days.

Nutrition Facts for 1 Serving

Calories: 170 Kcal, Protein: 10 g, Fat: 6 g, Carbohydrates: 22 g, Sugar: 4 g, Sodium: 419 mg, Cholesterol: 55 mg.

VEGETABLE PEEL CRISPS

🕐 25 Min   🍴 4 Servings

Ingredients

- 1 small sweet potato
- 1 parsnip
- 1 carrot
- 1 beetroot
- 1 teaspoon of fine sea salt
- 1/4 teaspoon of mixed herbs (optional)
- 1/4 teaspoon of coarsely ground black pepper
- Unflavored spray oil (such as sunflower)

Cooking Instructions

1. Scrub and dry vegetables. Slice thinly, about 3mm thick.
2. Pat slices dry, season with half the salt, pepper, and herbs (optional).
3. Preheat air fryer to 355°F (180°C). Arrange vegetables on the tray, spray with oil, and cook for 15-16 minutes, shaking every 5 minutes.
4. Combine remaining seasoning. Toss cooked vegetables with the mixture and cool on a baking sheet.
5. Serve and enjoy your Vegetable Peel Crisps!

Useful Tips

Store the crisps at room temperature in a cool, dry place. Avoid storing them in direct sunlight or near sources of heat to prevent them from becoming stale or soggy.

Nutrition Facts for 1 Serving

Calories: 443 Kcal, Protein: 2 g, Fat: 1 g, Carbohydrates: 20 g, Sugar: 9 g, Sodium: 254 mg, Cholesterol: 56 mg.

NACHOS

🕐 20 Min   🍴 4 Servings

Ingredients

- 2 cups of shredded cheese
- 2-3 cups of tortilla chips
- 1/2 cup of chopped tomatoes
- 1/4 cup of black and green olives
- 1/4 cup of yellow corn
- 1/4 cup of chopped jalapenos (optional)
- 2 tablespoons of chopped cilantro (optional)

Cooking Instructions

1. Spread the tortilla chips in a single layer in the air fryer basket, ensuring they overlap slightly to eliminate any gaps between the chips.
2. Cover the chips with half of the cheese.
3. Put the next layer of chips. Top over with remaining cheese, olives, cilantro, and jalapenos.
4. Put the basket inside the air fryer and fry it at 320°F for 3-5 minutes until the cheese is melted.
5. Remove it from the basket and top with chopped tomatoes.
6. Serve with guacamole. Enjoy your Nachos!

Useful Tips

Correctly overlapped chips prevent the cheese from dripping through the tray. The close arrangement of the chips helps create a stable base and ensures that the cheese and any other toppings stay on top of the chips during the cooking process.

Nutrition Facts for 1 Serving

Calories: 527 Kcal, Fat: 34 g, Carbohydrates: 59 g, Protein: 19 g, Sodium: 726 mg, Cholesterol: 59 mg.

FRIED CHEESE STICKS

🕐 2 Hours   🍴 24 Sticks

Ingredients

- 12 mozzarella cheese strings, cut in half
- 1 large beaten egg
- 1/2 cup of plain bread crumbs
- 1/2 cup of all-purpose flour
- 1/2 cup of ranch dressing, for serving
- 1/2 cup of marinara sauce, for serving
- 1 1/2 teaspoons of Italian seasoning
- 1/4 pinch of salt
- Ground black pepper, to taste

Cooking Instructions

1. Cut each mozzarella stick in half, spread them on a parchment-lined baking sheet, and flash freeze for 20 minutes.
2. Once they are frozen, cover each stick with the flour and dip into the egg with a fork.
3. After flash-freezing the mozzarella halves, roll them in the seasoned breadcrumbs until thoroughly coated. Place them back onto the baking sheet and freeze for 45 minutes or more.
4. Spray oil inside the basket and preheat it to 400°F. Spray the first batch of mozzarella sticks with some oil and place them inside the basket. Air fry at 400°F for 4-6 minutes until crispy and golden. Cook another batch.
5. Serve warm with ranch dressing and marinara sauce. Enjoy Fried Cheese Sticks!

Useful Tips

Keep the leftovers in an airtight food container in a fridge for up to 3 days. Reheat them before serving.

Nutrition Facts for 1 Cheese Sticks

Calories: 87 Kcal, Protein: 4 g, Carbohydrates: 5 g, Fat: 6 g, Sodium: 211 mg, Cholesterol: 16 mg.

CRISPY FALAFEL

🕐 37 Min   🍴 18 Servings

Ingredients

- 1 cup of dried chickpeas
- 1/2 cup of fresh parsley, roughly chopped
- 1/2 cup of fresh cilantro, roughly chopped
- 1 shallot
- 2 garlic cloves, minced
- 1 teaspoon of salt
- 1 teaspoon of cumin powder
- 1 teaspoon of coriander powder
- 1 teaspoon of cayenne pepper powder
- 1/4 teaspoon of baking soda
- Black pepper to taste

Cooking Instructions

1. Soak chickpeas in water for 24 hours, then drain and pat dry.
2. Blend chickpeas and ingredients until semi-fine. Chill for 1 hour.
3. Shape the mixture into balls with an ice cream scoop.
4. Spray your air fryer basket with oil. Cook patties at 375°F (190°C) for 16-18 minutes, flipping at 10 minutes.
5. Serve with tahini sauce. Enjoy your Crispy Falafel!

Useful Tips

Be sure to soak the dried chickpeas for 24 hours before using.

Store them in an airtight container in the refrigerator for up to 4-5 days.

Nutrition Facts for 6 Falafels

Calories: 46 Kcal, Protein: 12 g, Fat: 1 g, Carbohydrates: 8 g, Sugar: 1 g, Sodium: 151 mg, Cholesterol: 31 mg.

KALE CHIPS

🕐 15 Min   🍴 4 Servings

Ingredients

- 1 bunch of washed kale
- 2 tablespoons of olive oil
- 1 to 3 teaspoons of seafood seasoning
- Sea salt, to taste

Cooking Instructions

1. Preheat the air fryer to 375°F (190°C).
2. Remove the tough stems from the kale and tear the leaves into large pieces. Place the kale in a large bowl.
3. Add olive oil to the bowl and massage it into the leaves until evenly coated. Sprinkle the kale with seasoning and salt*.
4. Arrange the kale leaves in a single layer on a greased tray in the air fryer basket, working in batches if necessary.
5. Cook until the kale is crisp and just starting to brown, about 5-7 minutes. Let the kale stand for at least 5 minutes before serving.
6. Serve and enjoy your Kale Chips!

Useful Tips

*For added flavor, try tossing the kale in lemon juice before cooking for a bright, tangy taste, or use garlic salt for a savorier flavor.

For optimal taste, enjoy these kale chips fresh, but they can be stored in a well-sealed bag or container for 1 to 2 days.

Nutrition Facts for 1 Serving

Calories: 82 Kcal, Protein: 2 g, Fat: 7 g, Carbohydrates: 4 g, Sugar: 0 g, Sodium: 507 mg, Cholesterol: 0 mg.

DESSERTS

TENDER CREAM PUFFS

🕐 30 Min   🍴 12 Servings

Ingredients

- 1 cup of water
- 1/2 cup of unsalted butter
- 1/4 teaspoon of salt
- 1 cup of all-purpose flour
- 4 large eggs
- Whipped cream, for filling
- Powdered sugar, for dusting

Cooking Instructions

1. In a saucepan, bring water, butter, and salt to a boil over medium heat.
2. Add flour all at once; stir until a smooth ball forms. Remove from heat; let stand for 5 minutes.
3. Add eggs, one at a time, beating well after each addition. Continue beating until the mixture is smooth and shiny.
4. Drop by tablespoonfuls onto a greased air fryer basket.
5. Air fry at 355°F (180°C) for 15 minutes until golden brown. Cool on a wire rack.
6. Cut cream puffs in half, fill with cream and sliced fruit, top with the other half.
7. Serve and enjoy your Tender Cream Puffs!

Useful Tips

They can be stored in the refrigerator for up to 2-3 days.

Nutrition Facts for 1 Serving

Calories: 254 Kcal, Protein: 7 g, Fat: 30 g, Carbohydrates: 36 g, Sugar: 24 g, Sodium: 208 mg, Cholesterol: 145 mg.

TOASTER STRUDEL

🕐 9 Min   🍴 2 Strudels

Ingredients

- 2 frozen toaster strudels, any flavor
- 2 packets of toaster strudel icing (optional)
- Fresh fruit (optional)

Cooking Instructions

1. Preheat the air fryer to 350°F (175°C) and set the timer for 6 minutes.
2. Once preheated, place the toaster strudel in the air fryer.
3. Halfway through, flip the toaster strudel using tongs.
4. When done, remove the toaster strudel from the air fryer with tongs.
5. Top with the included icing and any additional toppings, such as fresh fruit.
6. Serve and enjoy your Toaster Strudel!

Useful Tips

Place the toaster strudels in a single layer.
If you have leftovers, store them in an airtight container in the fridge for up to 5 days.

Nutrition Facts for 1 Strudel

Calories: 198 Kcal, Protein: 2 g, Fat: 2 g, Carbohydrates: 35 g, Sugar: 14 g, Sodium: 165 mg, Cholesterol: 2 mg.

DONUTS

⏱ 17 Min 🍴 8 Donuts

Ingredients

- 4-5 tablespoons of milk, whole or low fat
- 2 cups of powdered sugar
- 1 teaspoon of vanilla extract
- 2 tablespoons of melted butter (salted or unsalted)
- 1 can (8 ounces) of flaky layers or buttermilk biscuits

Cooking Instructions

1. Open the biscuit can, cut out 1-inch holes in the centers, and set aside.
2. Brush the tops of the biscuits with melted butter using a pastry brush, then flip them over and brush the other side. It helps the biscuits brown and gives them a more pastry-like taste.
3. Preheat your air fryer to 355°F (180°C) for 2-3 minutes.
4. Place biscuits in a single layer, leaving space for rising.
5. Fry the donuts for 6-7 minutes, flipping halfway through. They are done when they have risen significantly and are golden brown.
6. Serve and enjoy your Donuts!

Useful Tips

Leftovers can be stored in an airtight container at room temperature for 1-2 days.

Nutrition Facts for 1 Donut

Calories: 189 Kcal, Protein: 1 g, Fat: 5 g, Carbohydrates: 35 g, Sugar: 28 g, Sodium: 142 mg, Cholesterol: 9 mg.

NUTELLA GRANOLA

⏱ 55 Min 🍴 8 Servings

Ingredients

- 2 1/2 cups of old-fashioned oats
- 1/2 cup of whole almonds
- 1/2 cup of semi-sweet chocolate chips
- 1/4 cup of Nutella
- 2 tablespoons of vegetable oil
- 2 tablespoons of pure maple syrup
- 1 tablespoon of heavy cream
- 1/8 teaspoon of salt

Cooking Instructions

1. Combine oats, almonds, and chocolate chips in a bowl.
2. Heat oil, heavy cream, Nutella, salt, and maple syrup in a saucepan until chocolate syrup forms.
3. Pour the chocolate mixture over the dry ingredients and stir to coat well.
4. Spread the mixture in an air fryer basket and press gently.
5. Air fry at 320°F (160°C) for 13-15 minutes until crispy.
6. Cool granola for 30 minutes and break it into pieces.
7. Serve and enjoy your Nutella Granola!

Useful Tips

You can substitute the chocolate chips with another type of chocolate, such as morsels, mini chocolate chips, or white chocolate chips.

After completely cooling, store it in an air-tight container for 5 days.

Nutrition Facts for 1 Serving

Calories: 297 Kcal, Protein: 6 g, Fat: 15 g, Carbohydrates: 34 g, Sugar: 13 g, Sodium: 40 mg, Cholesterol: 2 mg.

NUTELLA COOKIES

🕐 15 Min   🍴 32 Servings

Ingredients

- 1 3/4 cups of Nutella
- 1 cup of all-purpose flour
- 2 large eggs

Cooking Instructions

1. Combine the Nutella, flour, and eggs in a mixing bowl.
2. Line your air fryer basket with parchment paper. Scoop the prepared butter onto the parchment paper, leaving some space between each cookie.
3. Bake it at 340°F for 4 minutes until cooked through.
4. Serve and enjoy your Nutella Cookies!

Useful Tips

It is recommended to bake cookies in batches. Don't overcrowd the basket.

You can store the leftovers in an airtight food container at room temperature for up to 3 days.

Nutrition Facts for 1 Cookie

Calories: 82 Kcal, Protein: 1 g, Fat: 4 g, Carbohydrates: 10 g, Sugar: 6 g, Sodium: 9 mg, Cholesterol: 12 mg.

CARAMELIZED PEACHES

🕐 15 Min   🍴 4 Servings

Ingredients

- 4 peaches*
- 3 tablespoons of brown sugar
- 3 tablespoons of butter
- 2 teaspoons of olive oil
- 1 teaspoon of ground cinnamon

Cooking Instructions

1. Preheat your air fryer to 350°F.
2. Mix the butter, sugar, and cinnamon in a small bowl.
3. Wash, dry, and cut the peaches* in half, removing the pits. Drizzle the cut side of the peaches with olive oil.
4. Put the peach halves inside the preheated basket and air fry them at 350°F for 5 minutes.
5. Take a spoonful of the butter mixture and add it to the peaches. Continue cooking for 5-6 minutes more until the fruits are caramelized on top.
6. Serve with granola, nuts, and ice cream on top. Enjoy your Caramelized Peaches!

Useful Tips

* I strongly recommend cooking only from fresh peaches instead of canned or frozen.

You can keep the leftovers in an airtight food container in a fridge for up to 3 days. Just reheat at 350°F for 1-2 minutes before serving.

Nutrition Facts for 2 Peach Halves

Calories: 208 Kcal, Protein: 2 g, Fat: 14 g, Carbohydrates: 21 g, Sugar: 21 g, Sodium: 4 mg, Cholesterol: 31 mg.

CINNAMON ROLLS

🕐 50 Min   🍴 8 Rolls

Ingredients

- 1 can refrigerated cinnamon rolls with icing

Cooking Instructions

1. Preheat air fryer to 350°F (175°C).
2. Place cinnamon rolls in the air fryer basket, leaving space between each.
3. Air fry for 8-10 minutes, until golden brown and cooked through.
4. Remove from the air fryer and drizzle with the included icing.
5. Serve warm and enjoy your Cinnamon Rolls!

Useful Tips

Arrange the cinnamon rolls in the air fryer basket or on parchment paper with enough space between them to allow for expansion.
Cinnamon rolls can remain fresh for up to 1 week if stored in the refrigerator.

Nutrition Facts for 1 Roll

Calories: 140 Kcal, Protein: 2 g, Fat: 5 g, Carbohydrates: 24 g, Sugar: 9 g, Sodium: 340 mg, Cholesterol: 78 mg

POP-TARTS

🕐 18 Min   🍴 9 Servings

Ingredients

- 1 package of pie crust, refrigerated
- 1/2 cup of strawberry jam
- 2 tablespoons of water, for sealing
  For the Glaze:
- 3/4 cup of powdered sugar
- 2 tablespoons of milk
- 1 teaspoon of vanilla extract

Cooking Instructions

1. Lightly flour a surface and rolling pin. Roll out the pie crust into a rectangle and cut it into smaller rectangles. Spread jam on one, avoiding the edges. Wet edges, place another on top, press, and seal with a fork. Ventilate the top with small holes.
2. Preheat your air fryer to 355°F (180°C) and spray it with nonstick. Place the pop tarts inside, leaving space. Air fry for 8 minutes until golden. Repeat for all.
3. Mix powdered sugar, milk, and vanilla to make a glaze; adjust consistency. Once cooled, spoon the glaze over the pop-tarts and add sprinkles. Serve and enjoy Pop-Tarts!

Useful Tips

Ensure you don't overfill the pop-tarts with jam to prevent them from oozing out during cooking and let them cool slightly before adding the glaze.
They can be kept in the fridge for up to 3-4 days.

Nutrition Facts for 1 Serving

Calories: 318 Kcal, Protein: 3 g, Fat: 13 g, Carbohydrates: 47 g, Sugar: 19 g, Sodium: 208 mg, Cholesterol: 1 mg.

APPLE TURNOVERS

🕐 25 Min   🍴 4 Servings

Ingredients

- 2 medium apples, peeled, cored, and cubed
- 1 sheet of frozen puff pastry
- 1 egg
- 1 tablespoon of butter
- 2 tablespoons of brown sugar or honey
- 1 teaspoon of cinnamon
- 1/4 teaspoon of nutmeg
- 1/2 tablespoon of lemon juice
- 2 tablespoons of water
- Glaze, optionally

Cooking Instructions

1. In a saucepan, cook butter and apples until softened, about 5 minutes. Stir in brown sugar, honey, cinnamon, nutmeg, and lemon juice; simmer for 3 minutes until caramelized.
2. Cut puff pastry into 4 squares. Place 1/4 of the apple mixture on each square, brush edges with egg wash, fold over, seal with a fork, and brush tops with egg wash. Cut three slits in the tops.
3. Preheat the air fryer to 350°F (175°C) for 3 minutes. Arrange turnovers in the basket, not overlapping, and cook for 12-15 minutes until golden. Cool slightly on a wire rack. Drizzle with glaze.
4. Serve and enjoy your Apple Turnovers!

Useful Tips

Store in the refrigerator for up to 3-4 days.

Nutrition Facts for 1 Serving

Calories: 481 Kcal, Protein: 6 g, Fat: 27 g, Carbohydrates: 54 g, Sugar: 23 g, Sodium: 206 mg, Cholesterol: 41 mg.

BISCUITS

🕐 20 Min   🍴 6 Servings

Ingredients

- 2 cups of all-purpose flour
- 6 tablespoons of cold butter, cut into small pieces*
- 3/4 cup of milk
- 1 tablespoon of baking powder
- 1 teaspoon of granulated sugar
- 1/2 teaspoon of kosher salt

Cooking Instructions

1. Combine flour, baking powder, sugar, salt. Blend butter till crumbs.
2. Gradually add the milk and stir until a soft dough forms, being careful not to overmix.
3. Turn onto floured surface, knead, roll 1-inch thick, cut rounds.
4. Preheat air fryer to 320°F (160°C), if needed. Place biscuits, spaced. Air fry 8-10 mins till golden. Serve warm with butter or jam. Enjoy Biscuits!

Useful Tips

* Cold butter is essential for achieving flaky layers in biscuits.
Allow the leftover biscuits to cool to room temperature, then store them in an airtight container. They will keep in the refrigerator for 2-3 days.

Nutrition Facts for 1 Serving

Calories: 274 Kcal, Protein: 5 g, Fat: 13 g, Carbohydrates: 34 g, Sugar: 2 g, Sodium: 508 mg, Cholesterol: 34 mg.

CRANBERRY MUFFINS

🕐 25 Min   🍴 4 Muffins

Ingredients

- 1 large egg
- 1/4 cup of Greek yogurt
- 1/4 cup of fresh cranberries, chopped in half
- 1/2 cup of almond flour
- 3 tablespoons of sweetener
- 2 tablespoons of water
- 2 tablespoons of coconut flour
- 2 tablespoons of unflavored whey protein powder (or egg white powder)
- 2 teaspoons of orange zest
- 3/4 teaspoon of baking powder
- 1/4 teaspoon of vanilla extract
- 1/4 teaspoon of orange extract
- 1/8 teaspoon of salt

Cooking Instructions

1. Combine yogurt, egg, water, sweetener, vanilla extract, orange zest, and orange extract in a bowl.
2. Mix in almond flour, coconut flour, whey protein, baking powder, salt, and chopped cranberries.
3. Divide into 4 muffin cups.
4. Air fry at 310°F (155°C) for 15-18 mins till golden and firm.
5. Cool, then serve Cranberry Muffins!

Useful Tips

When combining the wet and dry ingredients, mix just until combined.
Store at room temperature for up to 2-3 days.

Nutrition Facts for 1 Muffin

Calories: 150 Kcal, Protein: 8 g, Fat: 6 g, Carbohydrates: 7 g, Sugar: 4 g, Sodium: 345 mg, Cholesterol: 78 mg.

PEANUT BUTTER COOKIES

🕐 30 Min   🍴 4 Servings

Ingredients

- 6 tablespoons of cold butter, cut into small
- 1 cup of creamy peanut butter
- 1/3 cup of packed light brown sugar
- 1/3 cup of semisweet chocolate chips
- 1 large egg
- 1 teaspoon of pure vanilla extract
- 1/2 teaspoon of baking soda
- Pinch of kosher salt

Cooking Instructions

1. Beat the egg in a medium bowl until smooth. Add the peanut butter, brown sugar, vanilla, salt, and baking soda; mix until combined and slightly thick, about 15 seconds.
2. Fold in chocolate chips. Roll into 1-inch balls, flatten to 1 1/2-inch disks.
3. Line your air fryer basket with foil, leaving an overhang. Arrange cookies 1/2 inch apart.
4. Air fry at 355°F (180°C) for 5-7 mins until deeply browned. Carefully remove foil with cookies, and let cool on a rack until firm, about 5 mins.
5. Transfer to rack to cool completely.
6. Enjoy Peanut Butter Cookies!

Useful Tips

Store the cookies at room temperature for up to 1 week.

Nutrition Facts for 1 Serving

Calories: 91 Kcal, Protein: 3 g, Fat: 6 g, Carbohydrates: 6 g, Sugar: 5 g, Sodium: 37 mg, Cholesterol: 8 mg.

CINNAMON APPLE CHIPS

🕐 35 Min 　　　 🍴 1 Serving

Ingredients

- 1 large apple
- 1 teaspoon of cinnamon
- 1 teaspoon of avocado or olive oil

Cooking Instructions

1. Slice an apple into 1/8-inch thick pieces using a mandoline slicer or knife. Remove seeds and stems. Toss slices with cinnamon and oil, applying both evenly. Preheat the air fryer to 300°F for 2 minutes.
2. Place apple slices in the air fryer basket. Cook at 300°F (150°C). for 20-25 minutes, flipping and rotating every 5 minutes, until fully dried with no wet spots. If chips start burning, reduce the temperature by 25°F.
3. Increase air fryer temperature to 325°F (165°C). Cook for 4-8 minutes, flipping and shaking every 90 seconds to 2 minutes, until crisp. Adjust the temperature if needed. Remove chips that brown quickly.
4. Let the chips cool for 5 minutes before enjoying. For maximum crispiness, serve within 10-20 minutes. Enjoy your Cinnamon Apple Chips!

Useful Tips

They will stay in a container for up to 5 days at room temperature but may soften overnight.

Nutrition Facts for 1 Serving

Calories: 126 Kcal, Protein: 0 g, Fat: 5 g, Carbohydrates: 24 g, Sugar: 0 g, Sodium: 122 mg, Cholesterol: 12 mg.

CANNOLI

🕐 25 Min 　　　 🍴 12 Servings

Ingredients

- 12 cannoli shells (store-bought or homemade)
- 1 cup of ricotta cheese, drained
- 1/2 cup of powdered sugar, plus extra for dusting
- 1/2 teaspoon of vanilla extract
- 1/4 cup of mini chocolate chips
- 1/4 cup of chocolate shavings
- Cooking spray

Cooking Instructions

1. Preheat the air fryer to 350°F (175°C).
2. Mix ricotta cheese, powdered sugar, and vanilla extract until smooth. Stir in mini chocolate chips.
3. Spray cannoli shells lightly with cooking spray. Place them in the air fryer basket, not overlapping.
4. Air fry for 4-5 minutes, until shells are golden and crispy.
5. Remove shells and let them cool slightly. Pipe the ricotta filling into each shell from both ends.
6. Dip the ends of the filled cannoli into chocolate shavings. Dust with powdered sugar.
7. Serve and enjoy your Cannoli!

Useful Tips

Store the cooled cannoli shells in an airtight container. They can stay fresh for up to 1 week.

Nutrition Facts for 1 Serving

Calories: 426 Kcal, Protein: 7 g, Fat: 29 g, Carbohydrates: 34 g, Sugar: 16 g, Sodium: 275 mg, Cholesterol: 55 mg.

BROWNIES

🕐 35 Min   🍴 4 Servings

Ingredients

- 1/4 cup of butter, melted and cooled slightly
- 1 large egg
- 1/3 cup of granulated sugar
- 1/3 cup of cocoa powder
- 1/4 cup of all-purpose flour
- 1/4 teaspoon of baking powder
- Pinch of salt

Cooking Instructions

1. Grease a 6-inch round cake pan with cooking spray. In a medium bowl, whisk together sugar, cocoa powder, flour, baking powder, and salt.
2. In a small bowl, whisk together melted butter and egg until combined. Add the wet ingredients to the dry ingredients and stir until mixed.
3. Pour the brownie batter into the prepared cake pan and smooth the top. Cook in the air fryer at 355°F (180°C) for 16-18 minutes. Let cool for 10 minutes before slicing.
4. Serve and enjoy your Brownies!

Useful Tips

Store the covered brownies in the refrigerator for up to 2-3 days.

Nutrition Facts for 1 Serving

Calories: 115 Kcal, Protein: 2 g, Fat: 6 g, Carbohydrates: 14 g, Sugar: 8 g, Sodium: 133 mg, Cholesterol: 38 mg.

MOLTEN LAVA CAKES

🕐 15 Min   🍴 3 Servings

Ingredients

- 6 tablespoons of unsalted butter, cut into pieces
- 4 ounces of semi-sweet chocolate bar*
- 1 large egg
- 1 egg yolk
- 3 tablespoons of white sugar
- 3 tablespoons of all-purpose flour
- 1/2 teaspoon of vanilla extract
- Pinch of salt

Cooking Instructions

1. Grease three 6-ounce ramekins. Melt butter and chocolate in a microwave-safe bowl, stirring every 30 seconds until melted. Set aside.
2. In a large bowl, use an electric beater to blend egg, egg yolk, vanilla extract, and sugar until well mixed. Add flour, chocolate mixture and salt; stir until combined. Pour into ramekins, filling halfway.
3. Place ramekins in your air fryer basket and air fry at 375°F (190°C) for 8-10 mins. Use a thick dish towel to remove ramekins. Let the cakes cool in the ramekins for 1 min. Use a butter knife to loosen the cakes and turn them onto plates. Serve with whipped cream, berries, or powdered sugar. Enjoy Molten Lava Cakes!

Useful Tips

* Use high-quality semi-sweet or dark chocolate for the best results.
Store the covered lava cakes in the refrigerator for up to 2-3 days.

Nutrition Facts for 1 Serving

Calories: 526 Kcal, Protein: 6 g, Fat: 12 g, Carbohydrates: 36 g, Sugar: 26 g, Sodium: 31 mg.

CONCLUSION

Thank you for joining me on this culinary journey through the world of air frying. I hope this cookbook has provided you with a wealth of delicious recipes and practical tips to make the most out of your air fryer. This versatile appliance not only simplifies the cooking process but also helps you create healthier meals without compromising on flavor or texture.

Remember, the key to successful air frying is experimentation and practice. Don't be afraid to try new ingredients, adjust cooking times, and explore different flavors.

Thank you for choosing this cookbook as your companion on this culinary journey.

Happy air frying!

LEAVE A REVIEW

As an independent author with a small marketing budget, reviews are my livelihood on this platform. If you enjoyed this book, I'd appreciate it if you could leave your honest feedback. You can do it by clicking the link below.

I read EVERY single review because I love the feedback from MY readers!

Scan this QR-code and you will receive a link to the review page.

Thank you for staying with me!

RECIPE INDEX

Made in the USA
Monee, IL
12 October 2024

67793306R00044